# CONCILIUM

*concilium* 1992/2

# THE NEW EUROPE – A CHALLENGE FOR CHRISTIANS

Edited by

Norbert Greinacher and
Norbert Mette

SCM Press · London

April 1992

ISBN: 0334 03013 7

Typeset at The Spartan Press Ltd, Lymington, Hants
Printed by Mackays of Chatham, Kent

*Concilium*: Published February, April, June, August, October, December

# Contents

Editorial    Norbert Greinacher and Norbert Mette    vii

*Special Column*    xiii

I · Conversion    1

Annihilating the 'Other' – The Memory of the Victims    3
   JON SOBRINO

'Till They Have Faces': Europe as a Sexist Myth and the
   Invisibility of Women    12
   MARY GREY

The Christian West: Farewell to an Epoch-Making Vision    20
   OTTMAR JOHN

II · Challenge    35

'The Rich Keep Getting Richer' – Economic Justice for All    37
   WOLFGANG KESSLER

A New Peace Policy    47
   DIETER LUTZ

Foreigners as an Opportunity    57
   JACQUES AUDINET

What about the Garden? The Ecological Dimensions of the
   European Home    66
   LUKAS VISCHER

How Religious is Europe?    75
   JAN KERKHOFS

III · Quests    85

The New Europe – A Challenge for the Churches    87
   JACQUES GAILLOT

Freedom in Solidarity – The Rescue of Reason                    96
  JOHANN BAPTIST METZ
Beyond Foundationalism and Relativism: Hermeneutics
  and the New Ecumenism                                       103
  DAVID TRACY
The Commitment of the Conciliar Process                       112
  MARGA BÜHRIG

Contributors                                                  121

# Editorial

## I

The European Ecumenical Assembly met in Basel from 15–21 May 1989 under the slogan 'Peace with Justice'. This was the first time since the Reformation that delegates from all the Christian churches on this continent had met, in order, as the Final Statement put it, 'to examine together what the Holy Spirit is saying to the churches today', in the face of the 'deadly threat which confronts humankind today'. Regardless of the fact that since May 1989 hectic and far-reaching changes have taken place which the Ecumenical Assembly could not have foreseen and which went far beyond even the most hopeful expectations of the time, we owe to this assembly a serious of pioneering directions which deserve further consideration. Thus the results of the synod of the European Bishops, being held during autumn 1991 while this issue is being prepared, need among other things to be judged by the degree to which they take up and develop the ecumenical consensus which could be found in Basel over the challenges and tasks that arise over the present and future of Europe.

Granted, in a number of respects the Final Statement of the European Ecumenical Assembly falls short of the clear positions and options which were taken by the Catholic Church in Latin America at its episcopal conferences in Medellin (1968) and Puebla (1979). Marga Bührig explains some of the reasons for this in her article which concludes this issue. However, it is a hopeful sign that this did not mark the end of the ecumenical or conciliar process – which some among the church leaders wanted, and deliberately attempted to bring about. On the contrary, the Conference of European Churches (CEC) and the Council of the European Episcopal Conferences (CCEE) have agreed to work towards a Second European Ecumenical Assembly and also to convene this within the foreseeable future.

If any further considerations and actions are not to fall short of the awareness of the problems formulated in Basel, they must be governed by the following principles:

1. The responsibility of Christians for the present and future of Europe can only be worked out in ecumenical collaboration. Only if the Christian churches in Europe bear witness in what they do that both understanding and reconciliation are possible after centuries of divisions and splits and that a variety of traditions can be a means of mutual enrichment, so that unity and difference are no longer mutually exclusive, can they credibly become a 'sign and instrument . . . of unity among all men' (Vatican Council, *Lumen Gentium* 1) and make an original contribution to the shaping of a new Europe. Any beginnings of a new confessionalism will waste this possibility and in the last resort encourage the process of de-Christianization. In this context the Catholic Church in particular is required to take seriously the anxiety of other churches that it is aiming at a re-Catholicizing of Europe, and by intensified ecumenical openness to show that this anxiety is groundless.

2. The call for an 'evangelization' or even a 're-evangelization of Europe' is a legitimate concern to the degree that it is remembered that the gospel call for conversion must always first be addressed to the churches and Christians (cf. *Evangelii nuntiandi*, 1975, 12). The delegates in Basel bore impressive witness to what that means by prefacing their remarks on the 'way to tomorrow's Europe' with a confession of sins in which they expressed before God and their fellow men and women their own individual and collective failures:

— We have failed because we have not borne witness to God's care and love for each and every creature and because we have not developed a life style which corresponds to our understanding of ourselves as God's creation.
— We have failed because we have not overcome the divisions among the churches and because we have often misused the authority and power given to us to strengthen false and limited solidarities like racism, sexism and nationalism.
— We have failed because we have caused wars and not exhausted all possibilities of committed mediation and reconciliation. We have excused wars and often too easily justified them too easily.
— We have failed because we have not questioned decisively enough political systems which misuse power and wealth, exploit the natural resources of the world only for their own benefit, and perpetuate poverty and marginalization.
— We have failed because we have regarded Europe as the centre of the world and have felt superior to other parts of the world.
— We have failed because we have not borne constant witness to the

sanctity and dignity of all life and the respect that we owe equally to all human beings, and the need to give all human beings the possibility of exercising their rights (no. 43).

3. This failure at the same time indicates the consequences which follow from the forgiveness prayed for to God and hoped for from God: they are aimed at a conversion, a conversion away from ourselves to what the Vatican II Pastoral Constitution *Gaudium et Spes* calls 'the joy and hope, the grief and anguish of the men of our time, especially those who are poor or afflicted in any way' (no. 1). Some of the concrete signs of this are noted by the Final Statement from Basel:

Conversion to God (*metanoia*) today means the obligation to look for a way:
— to a society in which human beings have equal rights and live together in solidarity.
— to a plurality of cultures, traditions and peoples in Europe.
— to a renewed society of men and women in church and society, in which at all levels both women and men bear equal responsibility and to which they can freely contribute their gifts, insights, values and experiences.
— to a fellowship of human beings with all creatures, in which the rights and integrity of these creatures are respected.
— to a community which is aware that it needs constant forgiveness and renewal, and which together thanks and praises God for his love and his gifts.

4. As the section we have just quoted expresses in a very evocative way, it would be foolish to claim that we have well-tried solutions to hand for all the problems which confront us. Rather, given an uncertain future, what we have are more like quests, guided by a concern to adopt an open and sensitive attitude to the changes which are taking place. In discerning and interpreting the 'signs of the time', Christians and churches are directed towards co-operation in solidarity with all those who are consistently working towards a really new Europe. In this respect, too, the Basel document has an impressive openness: in the image of a 'common European home' (cf. nos. 66ff.) it takes up a vision which was developed not in church circles but by the then General Secretary of the Soviet Communist Party and President of the Soviet Union, Mikhail Gorbachev. The power for change that can be generated if such collaboration is put into practice has been shown by the rapid social revolution in Central and Eastern Europe; it essentially stems from an alliance of different forces of

social reform which have been given active support not least from the ranks of the Protestant churches. These experiences of co-operation in solidarity could now help to shape the churches throughout Europe, as they seek a political and cultural role in societies which are becoming pluralist and democratic. All this, however, presupposes that similar democratic and subsidiaristic, federalistic structures also find a place in the churches – especially in the Catholic Church.

5. It does not require a great deal of imagination to see the number of churchgoers in the Europe of the future declining rather than growing, thus producing the situation which Karl Rahner already soberly forecast more than twenty years ago, namely that Christianity will find itself in a Diaspora situation. At least some of the delegates in Basel may have been aware of this. Nevertheless – and there is a further lesson here – they saw no reason to complain about this development or to greet it with resignation. Quite consistently, they took seriously the fact that the church must allow its agenda to be shaped by the acute problems of the world and that here its contribution would be not so much a matter of quantitative expansion as of qualitative commitment.

6. What are to be derived from the gospel are not the concrete forms of this commitment – that is a question for practical reason – but its perspectives and options. That clearly means that the churches and Christians have to seek their place less among the powerful than among the helpless, and as a priority ensure that the helpless get a hearing and are involved in the shaping of a new Europe. Such solidarity with the poor and the helpless cannot stop either at the frontiers of the old Europe or at those of a new Europe. The Basel delegates endorsed this universal orientation of their Christian obligation by stating that God's covenant with us and all creation is matched by a loyalty to this covenant in the face of which all other loyalties (whether to state, culture or social group) are secondary (cf. no. 77). However, there was a good example of just how difficult it is to put such verbal obligations into practice at the next significant event of the conciliar progress, the Assembly for Justice, Peace and the Integrity of Creation in Seoul in March 1990. Here the delegates from the churches in Europe in particular found the vehement demands for social justice made by the delegates from the churches of the 'Third World' difficult to take (there will be more about this in the article by Martha Bührig). The experiences of Seoul make it abidingly clear that a new Europe, a common European home, can be achieved only to the degree that at the same time there is universal concern for a habitable earth.

## II

It is natural for the present issue of *Concilium*, the subject of which is 'The New Europe – a Challenge for Christians', to take up the principles and options noted by the European Ecumenical Assembly and attempt to develop them further. This concern has also determined the choice of topics within the issue, since it was impossible to discuss all the aspects involved.

So the first block of themes begins with the call for conversion. That comes about by deliberately listening to the voices of others, the voices of those who for a long time have tended to be overlooked in Europe and who risk continuing to be overlooked in the future. In his prophetic and utopian reflections Jon Sobrino urgently presents the perspective of those for whom Europe has anything but good connotations; impoverished and exterminated down the centuries, they risk being completely overwhelmed by the economic and political developments which are imposing them- selves with increasing vigour. Mary Grey unmasks the sexist myth bound up with talk of Europe and calls for a re-reading of European history in which all those who have so far been kept hidden on the shadow side make an appearance. Finally, by means of reconstructions of former ideas of 'the West', Ottmar John engages in a criticism of a view of Europe which has been influential over the last two centuries, particularly in the Catholic sphere.

The concern of the second block of themes is to identify in detail and analyse the social, economic, cultural and political challenges which are becoming increasingly urgent in Europe, at present and for the future, and to develop viable strategies for action. Here Wolfgang Kessler takes up the question of economic justice in view of the ever-increasing gulf between poor and rich, both all over the world and in Europe itself; Dieter S. Lutz sketches the basic outlines of an 'order of mutual peace' to take account of the change in the threats facing Europe; Jacques Audinet uses the treatment of foreigners (refugees, those seeking asylum, immigrants, etc.) as a criterion for whether a new Europe is really being formed; and finally Lukas Vischer discusses the ecological dimension of the 'European home'. Common to all these contributions is that they not only make a clear analysis of the particular situation (crisis), but also discuss viable conceptions and strategies for future action, not least calling on Christians and the churches to play an active part in them. Jan Kerkhofs discusses what effects the process of modernization in Europe has had and is having on religious attitudes and practices, using evidence selected from the most recent empirical investigations, which are being carried out on a trans-national basis; they demonstrate quite clearly that the Diaspora situation of Christianity forecast by Karl Rahner is already largely becoming a reality.

Against this background, the question becomes more acute what fundamental directions can and should be normative for action by Christians and the churches in the light of the present and future situation of Europe and its global context. The contributions to the third block of themes represent an invitation to appropriate quests. 'Being the church in Europe today', 'constant conversion', and 'in planetary dimensions' are the key phrases in Bishop Jacques Gaillot's noteworthy contribution. They also keep emerging both in the remarks by Johann Baptist Metz, who recalls the other, long-neglected side of a European spirit aware of its Christian roots and its determining features pointing forward to the future, and calls for the redemption of these roots; and in David Tracy's plea for a thoroughgoing revision of what has hitherto been a Eurocentric epistemology in the direction of a hermeneutic which takes account of its social location, and a new ecumenical understanding which makes it possible to deal productively with the formation of a multicultural and multireligious society – beyond fundamentalism and relativism. Both contributions also explicitly bring out that perspective which is the subject of Jon Sobrino's urgent admonition and runs like a scarlet thread right through the issue: the decisive criterion of whether a new Europe is really beginning with 1992 will be whether a lasting change is taking place in the way in which Europeans deal with others. Will they be discovered and recognized as others, rather than being conquered and annihilated, or assimilated to Europe's own concerns?

Norbert Greinacher
Norbert Mette

# 1962–1992
# Vatican II – Thirty Years After

*Concilium* was born in the climate of Vatican II and set out to continue the experience of collaboration between theologians and of service within the community of the church in the perspective of the spiritual, cultural and institutional renewal promoted by the Council. Today in 1992, thirty years after the opening of this great conciliar assembly, it is worth asking ourselves what is the present state of awareness of the Council, its consequences and its significance. The enthusiasm which characterized the expectation and the celebration of Vatican II is spent. The generation of those directly involved is disappearing; even the blaze of rejection prompted by Lefebvre has turned into a melancholy smouldering. It is clear that the historical context has changed profoundly, to a marked degree not least as a result of the conciliar celebration itself.

During the past three decades various ways of reading Vatican II have crystallized. The inspiration behind them is essentially ideological rather than historical.

The most radical reading is that of the 'integralists'. According to them, Vatican II was dominated by maximalism and therefore marks a break in the continuity of post-Tridentine Catholic tradition. According to this point of view the Council was a mistake.

At the opposite extreme, some suggest reading Vatican II as an endorsement of positions and orientations diametrically opposed to those dominant within Roman Catholicism in the last decades before Vatican II itself. Thus the decisions of the Council are read mirror-fashion in conjunction with the ecclesiastical *magisterium* before 1960. Vatican II, still Eurocentric and dogmatizing, was the end of an era, and had already been overtaken by the facts.

According to many others, Vatican II is a 'minor' council, given the lack of dogmatic definitions, condemnations and anathematizations. Its 'pastoral' character is understood to put it on a lower level, above all a lower level than the other modern councils, Trent and Vatican I. Its uncertain and tortuous course caused the difficulties that arose after the Council; that makes it necessary for Rome to guide its reception, to filter the impulses which come from the Council itself.

Yet others, finally, suggest that Vatican II should be described as a 'transitional' council, a term originally used in connection with John XXIII. It is seen to be a 'transitional' council in the strong sense, since through it the church left the Tridentine era – or even the Constantinian era – and began on a new stage. So this is an event which marks a point of no return in the itinerary of Christianity lasting over many centuries.

The past years have seen the production of studies on individual decisions of the Council, or on some aspects of its development. However, these have always been publications which have had no organic commitment to follow through what has in fact happened as a result of the Council. The result has been to produce a fragmentary awareness of the work of the Council, leaving in the shade the global historical significance of Vatican II as an event making the passage of Catholicism, and to a large degree also of the whole of Christianity, from one era to an other. Moreover, the lack of an overall vision of the Council has meant that there has been no major stimulus towards a deeper understanding of doctrine in the direction of the renewal indicated or suggested by the Council itself. Here is a by no means insignificant reason for the uncertainties and *longeurs* of post-conciliar reception.

Thirty years on, Vatican II appears as an event which – over and above its limits and lacunas, and indeed despite them – has continued to keep alive the hope and optimism of the gospel. A tendency to linger over a view of the Council as the sum of hundreds of pages of texts – almost always prolix and sometimes ephemeral – has so far put a brake on perceiving its more fruitful significance, namely as a stimulus for the community of believers to accept a disturbing encounter with the word of God and with the mystery of human history. The Council did not intend to produce a new doctrinal 'summa' (according to John XXIII, 'a council did not meet for this') nor to respond to all the problems. It is always more vital to recognize the priority of the event of the Council even over its own decisions; these cannot be read as abstract normative dictates but must be seen as the expression and prolongation of the event itself. The commitment to renewal, the longing for research, openness to the gospel, brotherly concern for all men and women, which characterized Vatican II, are not aspects of its folklore or at any rate marginal and transient features.

On the contrary, this is the spirit of the conciliar event to which a healthy and correct hermeneutic of its decisions cannot fail to make reference.

So the time has come to bring about a historicization of Vatican II, not to push it further away, relegate it to the past, but to get beyond the controversial phase of its reception by the church. We have a duty to the new generations which did not experience the event of the Council to provide a tool which will allow a critically correct awareness of its significance in the present.

To reconstruct the phenomenology of the work of the Council and also the spirit and the dialectic which inspired and characterized the assembly, calls for an interweaving of an account of the work of the Council as it went on day by day with an account of the development of the awareness of the assembly and its various components. The great doctrinal, institutional and pastoral themes need also to be traced through their 'transverse' evolution, i.e. independently of the strict sequence of work on them. Equally, there is a need to reconstruct the dialectical relationship between the internal climate of the Council and the external context, not only in Rome but also wider afield.

Attention to Vatican II as an event rather than the implementation of an institutional model or a sum of the decisions produced raises the problem of developing adequate hermeneutical criteria. These must be distinct criteria – even if they are connected or complementary – relating to the canonical requirements of the institutional legitimacy of a council and the criteria for interpreting the corpus of its decisions.

It is obvious that this involves a reconstruction of the history of the Council on the basis of a rigorously critical analysis of the sources; all the sources that have been preserved: oral and written, official and informal, collective and individual, internal and external. The question to be answered is not, 'How did the corpus of the decisions of Vatican II come to be approved?', but rather, 'How did Vatican II in fact come about and what was its significance?'

It will be necessary to distinguish between the image the Council had of itself (its sense of itself and how this came over to contemporaries then) and the re-reading of the Council today, after the conclusion of its work and during its reception. On the other hand, the production of a history of the Council must necessarily take place during the period after the Council and must therefore be committed, by means of the rigorous use of the sources in all their complexity and the careful exercise of accurate criticism, to going back to the Council 'in itself' – not as an abstraction, but as a completely historical reality.

More than thirty years after the announcement of Vatican II (25 January

1959) and more than twenty-five years after the conclusion of its work (8 December 1965), it has seemed possible to set in motion a research project which is to take several years, aimed at the production of a history of the Council. The project is under the supervision of the Institute of Religious Sciences in Bologna, and is being co-ordinated by an international group of scholars. Over and above its apologetic or polemical aims, it plans to make a critically rigorous reconstruction of the conciliar event in all its dimensions, components and values, based on the sources and carried out with the historical method.

To this end, an intercontinental and interconfessional team is at work with the aim of achieving a well-balanced view not only of the complex development 'within' the work of the conciliar assembly, but also of the dialectical relationship with 'external factors' relating to the social, political, economic and cultural context on the various continents.

The research, backed up by documentary material of particular interest and numerous qualified collaborators, will produce exceptionally interesting results. Publication of the first volume – on the preparatory phase of the Council (1959–1962) should take place within a couple of years. Four other volumes will follow, each devoted to one of the sessions of the assembly.

Giuseppe Alberigo

# I · Conversion

# Annihilating the 'Other' – The Memory of the Victims

## Jon Sobrino

1992 recalls what has happened over the last five centuries in what is now Latin America and also celebrates the birth of a new Europe. On the first aspect, *Concilium* has issued a Special Number, *1492–1992: The Voice of the Victims*, to which I contributed 'The Crucified Peoples: Yahweh's Suffering Servant Today'.[1] Now I have been asked to write about the new Europe from the viewpoint of the 'annihilated' others and their memories as victims, and the truth is that I really have nothing very important to add to what I wrote then. I would ask the reader to look at both issues together, since the reality of Latin America, and of the whole Third World, is still the best hermeneutic for understanding the final truth of the new Europe.

Before going on, however, I have to confess to a feeling of impotence in trying, once again, to communicate what is obvious in the world of the victims, but becomes steadily less obvious in a world of abundance alien to them: what poverty, hope, life, death, commitment and martyrdom actually mean. So the tone of these lines is reflective rather than propositional. I have, I must add, been encouraged by writings such as those of J. B. Metz, who after travelling in Latin America could find nothing more poignant than a 'personal recollection', particularly his recollection of 'the faces of Latin America'.[2]

Finally, these lines are consciously prophetic and utopian, even though I know that in Europe both prophecy and utopia seem to have been replaced by tolerant acceptance of differences and fragmentation. Nevertheless, from the side of the victims, neither prophecy nor utopia can be discarded, since the 'other' is always their reserve in history.

## 1. The première of the New Europe and the Gulf War

Throughout history, the nations of Europe have fought among themselves and invaded, despoiled and annihilated the 'other', the Third World. Now it would seem that Europe has changed its spots and become a united, peaceful, free and democratic Europe, achieved not by means of war, but through negotiation and consensus. All this seems to be a good thing. But, as victims, we can ask whether this new Europe is also new in its relations with the Third World. In order to verify this, let us look at how it acted in the first major international challenge it has had to face, the Gulf War.

Without being simplistic, one can say that European actions in this as a whole have brought the following elements to light: 1. its habitual historical amnesia, 'the forgetfulness that nests in our modern consciousness',[3] about the origins of the conflict: the geo-political division of the area carried out some years ago by European powers; 2. its submission to US politics, failing to emerge as an effective alternative to the superpowers; 3. its material co-operation in men, arms, military equipment and financial resources to an act of frightful tragedy (think of the 80,000 air sorties flown over Iraq); 4. the moral legitimation it gave to a war that people sought to justify by hypocritical invocation of principles not observed in other similar or even clearer situations: harping on the injustice of the invasion of Kuwait while ignoring decades of US and Soviet invasions and interventions, the most recent being the US invasion of Panama in December 1989; ignoring major violations of human rights committed by governments against their populations, without any nation declaring war on them – certainly not the United States, which has lent decisive support to successive governments in Latin America which have assassinated, massacred, tortured and 'disappeared' hundreds of thousands of their subjects; ignoring the obligation to comply with United Nations resolutions, such as that imposing sanctions on the state of Israel; 5. its overriding concern for 'doing business', even with the now reviled government of Iraq, going so far as to provide this with the means of producing chemical and nuclear weapons; 6. and, finally, even though secularized Europe did not invoke God as the President of the United States did, it has shown the existence of idols in it – oil, the ultimate and untouchable – and shown this by the victims they have produced (not that these, maybe 100,000 in number, appeared much on the TV screens in the most televised war in history).

The legality or illegality of this war can be discussed *ad nauseam* in theoretical terms, but in terms of humanism and Christianity, in terms of the 'new Europe', which is what concerns us here, two things emerge clearly. The first is that Europe (and the whole of the North of the planet) has over centuries built up vast resources: religious, philosophical and ideological traditions, science and technology, capital . . . but this whole accumulation does not seem to have prepared it for dealing more humanely with the poor of this world or for resolving serious problems such as the Iraqi invasion in a different, just and human fashion. It would seem, then, that Europe has invented or discovered everything except brotherly love and justice. And if it seems surprising even to make this sort of observation, as if it were utopian lunacy to imagine that some nations can deal justly and compassionately with others, the fact is that from the standpoint of the victims, the new Europe looks much like the old. The second point is that, with or without secularization, in accordance with the reasoning of modernism or the non-reasoning of post-modernism, the idols are still as large as life: the final ('theologal', it might be called) decision to put the goal of maintaining and improving the 'standard of living' reached in Europe above any consideration of the life led by peoples in the Third World. Centuries ago this idol was gold: now it is oil or its equivalents. The means of getting them have changed, but the overriding decision to get them, secure them and keep them as personal property does not seem to have changed. And let us recall that Pope John Paul II – so applauded in much of Europe when he defends European unity and works for the fall of Communist regimes – was ignored when he raised his voice against the Gulf War.

Seen from the Third World, then, the new Europe is not as new as it seems, but its age-old self: inward-looking and self-interested, but forgetful and dis-interested – to the point of plunder and exploitation when necessary – in regard to the poor majorities of this world.

## 2. Dis-interest in the other

The new Europe seeks to maintain its own identity and distance itself from the United States and Japan, and now it can try to wash its hands of the ills that beset the Third World, assigning responsibility for these to the other superpowers. But this should not lead it to forget that, historically, its well-being is built on the mass of corpses and the impoverished of the Third World, to which the plight of so many immigrants over the past decades must be added. Although forms of oppression are no longer so direct, the Third World still does not interest Europe in itself; it is still 'the other', and not only as something distinct, still less as something complementary and enriching, but as something inferior, something to be utilized and if necessary oppressed: the despised other, which can even receive benefits from Europe, but never the other way round. This basic dis-interest is what still defines Europe's relationship to the Third World. Europe has no notion of and shows no feeling for the 'human family', or even for the 'human species' (which might have been expected in an age of ecological concern); it just knows and feels that 'we' are very different from 'the others'.

The new Europe does indeed claim that in due course it will take account of and work for justice in the Third World. There are two reasons for this: 1. because this will help to assure the long-term well-being of the North; 2. because terms such as 'justice' and 'the poor' have become part of the linguistic orthodoxy (though not the orthopraxis) of the developed world. But the truth is that the Third World is still not centrally present in Europe as a world of human beings; it is seen rather as an instrumental world (as though it had no existence in its own right), as a discovered world (as though it had not existed until Europe took notice of it), as a 'third' world (and so, naturally, coming after the other two).

The fact is, to put it mildly, that the poor of the world are simply not interesting. It is, of course, stated that the new Europe should be open to the Third World and its two or three thousand million poor, but that it will be once it itself has been consolidated. The poor of this world always come – if they come at all – 'after' the solution of any problems more urgent than that of massive poverty, whether such problems are the nuclear threat, global warming, European security . . . There is always something more important for the European 'us'. The poor, the 'others', must wait, although in reality they cannot wait any longer, since, far from going away, poverty is increasing, and can itself be the biggest threat to the well-being of the North.

At times, however, the poor are not merely told to wait; they are shamelessly manipulated. In the Gulf War, for example, the majority of US soldiers were recruited from among the ethnic minorities, hispanics and blacks. Spain has invested thousands of millions of pesetas to make political and economic capital out of 1992 at the expense of the memory of the victims. And so while at the Barcelona Olympics athletic records will be broken, in Latin America millions of human beings – this is not a rhetorical overstatement – will break records for hunger. And who knows if any of the present reality of Latin America – its poverty, violation of human rights, subjection to the United States – will be on show at the World Fair of Seville.

And after the fall of the Eastern bloc and the establishment of a 'new world order' things can get even worse. For the first time, the Third

World will be completely on its own, and its meaning will have changed, too, for the First World.

> The essence of the population of the Third World today, unlike a hundred years ago, is that it is, from the point of view of the First World and its economic needs, a superfluous population. The Third World, with its seas, air, nature, is still needed, even if only as a dumping-ground for toxic wastes, and its raw materials are still needed . . . What is no longer needed is the greater part of the population of the Third World.[4]

J. B. Metz is right: the North of the planet is experiencing a post-modernism that apart from 'again putting the so-called Third World at a faceless distance', is carrying out 'something like a cultural strategy of immunizing Europe', 'the cult of a new innocence', 'an attempt intellectually to avoid the global demands made on us', 'a new variant of . . . "tactical provincialism"'.[5]

## 3. Ignorance of the victims and culpable blindness

Egoistic disinterest is possible only through ignorance, but a degree of ignorance that amounts to culpable blindness. It might be supposed, really, that any normal persons of good will, in Europe or any other part of the world, would react in some way to the plight of the Third World given a minimum of knowledge of it. But they have no knowledge. Who in the new Europe knows how many millions of poor there are in it, if these are the exception, a minority, or the majority, thousands of millions, and thirty million of these die of hunger every year? Who knows the number of wars fought since the Second World War – more than a hundred, and all in the Third World, with victims numbered in the tens of millions?

Of course Europe gets news of the Third World; of course its television shows events such as the murder of the Jesuits in El Salvador and inevitably the Gulf War. But these are presented as news, not as reality, and the two things are not the same. Starving children in Ethiopia and beheaded peasants in El Salvador can be news for a time, but the deepest truth of the countries of the Third World does not become reality for viewers. News does not last for long, and since in our culture what is not communicated by the media is not real, once the news is over, it is as though the Third World with its poverty and its daily oppression ceases to exist. Furthermore, the communications industry tends to convert news into merchandise to be communicated strategically according to the reaction and audience envisaged. So in the long term, and often in the short, one news item is lost and drowned among others, and news items about the Third World often die the death of a thousand interpretations and the death of competing with other items that have nothing to do with them. Finally, news items about the Third World that should reinforce one another in fact seem to cancel one another out, so that the news of a massacre in Guatemala makes us forget the existence of millions of people in India blinded by lack of vitamins. And if all news items about the Third World are lumped together, they seem to produce a reaction of 'That's the way the world is', rather than protest and the decision to do something to change the way the world is.

Reality seeks to speak out, as Rahner said, and in a world that has become an electronic village, news should be its sacrament, but things do not work out like that. The wretched of the earth keep calling out and the blood of the victims still clamours to heaven, but Europe, old or new, goes on being unaware. We need to know why.

I began by saying – in Europe's defence – that from there it is practically impossible to know the radical otherness of the Third World. Europe now has no image – and therefore no concept – of the poverty and repression that rule in the Third World (though there should be some image and concept of their indignity, if Europe were capable of seeing the indignity to which it subjects so many immigrants . . .). What is happening in Europe is that life is now taken for granted, and life is precisely what can never be taken for granted in the Third World: it is what constitutes the greatest task. Life is the problem and the utopia, the minimum and the maximum, from which everything is viewed. So poverty is not just failing to reach the average standard of quality of life, but closeness to death, slow or violent. Then, from a historical and existential point of view, the *analogy* of basic concepts such as life and death, dignity and indignity, freedom and oppression, becomes, in practical terms, their *equivalence*. To say that 'all men are born equal, with the same rights and the same dignity' is simply not true from a historical point of view, since enjoyment of the possibilities of life, of rights and of dignity, depends on having been born in Berlin, Madrid or Rome instead of in Haiti, Biafra or Pakistan.

Having said this in Europe's defence, we also have to point to its lack of will to truth, to know the reality of the Third World, its culpable blindness. For Europe, the Third World is not only something unknown and difficult to get to know, but above all what is covered up and should not be uncovered. So there is not only ignorance about it; there are lies about it, too. At work here is the basic sinfulness that oppresses truth, in Paul's words, or the Devil, murderer and father of lies, in John's words.

Ignacio Ellacuría used to say that what 1492 discovered was not the reality of Latin America (which remained covered), but that of Europe (Spain and Portugal). This is still so today, and in this lies the root of its pretended ignorance, deliberate and blameworthy, about the Third World: it is the victims, like a mirror held upside down or the secretions that show a patient's state of health (both Ellacuría's similes), that show us our own reality. Put in simple terms, if in fact the victims are not hidden, but seen, they prevent us from stifling the great question: 'What have you done with your brother?' This is what Europe does not want to hear, and this is why it does not want to look at them.

## 4. A compassionate reasoning

In this situation, what Europe needs to be really 'new' is to turn back and help the victims. In theoretical terms, it needs a 'compassionate reasoning'. If it does not do this, its current debate on modernity and post-modernity will mean little to the victims.

Turning back to the victims means effectively going beyond Euro-centrism, something that will be difficult to achieve, since this has become second nature to Europe, both in its modernist and post-modernist forms. For modernity and its reasoning, nothing seemed to be real unless it had been filtered through Europe, and any different problems or situations in the Third World were seen as states previous to reality. So, to give two critical examples that affect theology: first, in the age of faith it seemed that God had come to the world via Europe, and had, thanks to Europe's generosity (its age-old traditions, missionaries, theologies, resources), then gone to the 'other' worlds. And when the age changes to one of loss of faith, the basic problems not only are but have to be secularization and atheism, since these are European problems. Second, for post-modernity and its special reasoning (or lack of it) it is not very sensible to speak of prophecy, let alone of utopia. Why not? For the simple reason that both seem to have failed in Europe, and therefore are not advisable. So in both cases, Eurocentrism: Europe is reality and reality is Europe. This is what needs to be radically transcended if Europe is to turn back to 'the other'.

And once turned back to the other, it has to exercise compassion toward the victims. From this standpoint, the debate on modernity and post-modernity in its present form is totally irrelevant if the victims of this world are not present in it as a central theme. In other words, we do not know which is better or worse: modernity with its reasoning which ended up as instrumental oppressive reasoning, or post-modernity with its non-reasoning which ends up being dis-interested reasoning. The fact is that without compassion there is no humanity, and without humanity there can be no human reasoning.

To put it another way: to wake from the dream of dogmatism and now from the dream of utopia is of little use if we do not also wake from the dream of inhumanity. We can debate *ad nauseam* what dreams we are victims of, and be thankful for the teachers who have made us suspect them and wake from them, and for the teachers who appeal to the realism of the possible and temper the flights of a reason that believes itself capable of everything. But such benefits turn to evils if they make us ignore the victims, to 'pass over' the deaths of the poor. 'In the end we get used to the crises over poverty in the world, which seem increasingly to be a permanent part of the scene, so that we shrug our shoulders and delegate them to an anonymous social evolution which has no subjects'.[6]

This is what I mean by compassionate reasoning, which can and even should incorporate some elements of both modernity and post-modernity, but without which neither one nor the other are human today, since the victims of this world are neither instruments nor incidental, but the central reality. In theological terms, I have formulated this as a request that it be understood above all as *intellectus misericordiae* (*amoris, justitiae, liberationis*).[7]

### 5. Utopia of the minimum-maximum: the life of the poor

If the very fact of mentioning utopia in the new Europe is in itself utopian, how much more utopian it is to give it a content: yet that has to be done, from both human and Christian standpoints. It is necessary for Europe, since Europe is threatened 'by the process of modernization which . . . increasingly acts as an automatic process'.[8] And it is necessary for the Third World, since without utopia not only will there be no fullness and quality of life, but there will simply not be life. The fact is that, in Mgr Romero's brilliant words, 'We have to defend the *minimum* which is the *maximum* gift of God: life'.

The victims of the Third World are the prophets who demand a compassionate reasoning, but they are also those who make a utopian reasoning possible, even though this may not seem to aim very high. As Ellacuría said: 'A civilization of poverty that would take the place of the present civilization of wealth . . . a civilization of work that would take the place of the dominant civilization of capital.'[9] This, then, is a utopia of the minimum for Europe, but it is also a utopia of the maximum – in quality, since it guarantees life to the poor, and in quantity, since it is what most of the world's population aspire to. And it is a utopia for all, since the effort to achieve a minimum of life for the poor brings austerity on one hand, but austerity shared on the other, and this is human fellowship.

It is the victims of the world who have made these reflections possible, since here we are still doing theology not *after*, but *in* Auschwitz. Let me say in conclusion that the crucified peoples are those who shed positive light on both prophecy and utopia. Ellacuría put it succinctly: 'The crucified people are the victims of the sin of the world and also those who will bring salvation to the world.'[10]

*Translated by Paul Burns*

## Notes

1. *Concilium* 1990/6, reissued 1991, 120–9.
2. 'With the Eyes of a European Theologian', ibid., 113–19. See also J. B. Metz and H. E. Bahr, *Augen für die Anderen. Lateinamerika, eine theologische Erfahrung*, Munich 1991. I quote Metz several times here to emphasize that what I say about the Third World is clear enough to anyone who approaches it with honourable intentions and good will.
3. Ibid., 114.
4. F. Hinkelammert, *La crisis del socialismo y el tercer mundo*, San José, 1991, 6.
5. Hinkelammert, *La crisis* (n. 4), 115.
6. Ibid.
7. 'Teología en un mundo sufriente. La teología de la liberaçion como "intellectus amoris"', *RLT* 15, 1988, 243–66.
8. Metz, 'With the Eyes' (n. 2), 117.
9. 'Utopía y protestismo', in I. Ellacuría and J. Sobrino (eds.), *Mysterium Liberationis* I, Madrid 1990, 425.
10. 'El pueblo crucificado', ibid., II, 215.

# 'Till They Have Faces': Europe as a Sexist Myth and the Invisibility of Women

## Mary Grey

### Introduction

The story is told that Caractacus, the British chieftain taken to Rome as captive in the reign of the Emperor Claudius (AD 51), on seeing the might and grandeur of ancient Roman palaces, exclaimed, 'You have all this, yet you covet our poor huts!'[1] For me this story functions as a parable for the European 'syndrome', since those who were once captive went on to be conquerors and exploiters of the dwellers of 'the poor huts' in lands outside Europe. More tragically, ever since the Emperor Constantine's famous vision of the cross in the skies and the prophecy, 'By this sign you will conquer',[2] a militarist ethic has been imposed on the world at large by Europeans in the name of Christianity itself.

This so-called 'seamless garment' of European culture which extends from the Caspian Sea to the south of Spain is in fact a sexist myth, built as it is on the invisibility and exclusion of women from its structures and foundational thinking. The earliest example of a European woman who found a prophetic voice but was condemned by the god (Apollo) as mad was Cassandra, princess of Troy at the time of the Trojan War. It is significant that her madness consisted in prophesying the imminent destruction of the nation through war: she was listened to as little as are the prophetic voices from peace movements today.[3]

'Europe' is a sexist myth, even if we take 'myth' in both the two current, common usages of the word. A myth is a narrative, a foundational symbolic story or set of stories through which a nation or cultural group within it understands and remembers its origins and evisions its 'end-times' in order to live life meaningfully in the present. But 'myth' is also currently used in the sense of 'half-truth', the false consciousness, or 'bad faith' induced by commercial advertising, ill-grounded popular opinions and a lazy accept-ance of fictitious ideas. In both these senses, the cultural construction which is Europe can be regarded as a sexist myth. In the foundational stories of Europe – the philosophical, psychological and scientific building blocks which underpin the formation of the European liberal democracy – women are either invisible, or defined in relation to men with certain severely restricted roles within the patriarchal household. Speaking about the lack of gender-awareness of fifth-century Europe, Peter Brown remarked that 'it is a comfortable and dangerous illusion to assume that, in much of the evidence, the presence of women is even *sensed*'.[4] Yet Virginia Woolf called attention to the fact that women appeared numerous times in the catalogue of the British Library, men not at all.[5] In other words, womens' presence consists in being written about, defined and controlled. Small wonder that the same writer cried 'As a woman I have no country!'[6]

It is one thing to be written out of the founding myths; it is another thing to be present as part of 'false consciousness', present as 'guilty Eve', as 'the Angel in the House', as witch, temptress and fertility goddess. The terrifying thought arises, given the prevalence of such false consciousness, that without such stereotypical female roles the whole cultural seamless garment would collapse like Alice in Wonderland's pack of cards! What has to be asked is, first, what part has Christian theology played in the construction of this sexist myth? And, secondly, can anything be salvaged from Europe's past as ingredient for a new myth? What creative remembrance will offer liberating possibilities for the way men and women relate – within Europe, and far beyond its boundaries?

## 1. Europe's monocultural myth

If we examine the philosophical and cultural movements and periods of European development, the so-called great landmarks of cultural progress, the dilemma becomes sharper. It is true that Plato allowed a few intelligent women within his Republic – because the philosophers needed to procreate. But Aristotle – as is well known – clearly excluded women from public life as 'a-political' and as 'misbegotten males'. What is not so often perceived is how movements such as the Renaissance and the Enlighten-ment are understood as focussing exclusively on Renaissance 'man' and male subjectivity. The French Revolution began by enthroning the Goddess of Reason in the Cathedral of Notre Dame, while at the same time excluding women from its aims of 'liberté, egalité and fraternité'. The

Romanticism of Goethe and Rousseau idealized and sentimentalized 'woman', ignoring the suffering of real women. Such idealization of feminine identity then made it easier to achieve the nineteenth-century split between the private and public worlds: the 'feminine' virtues of docility and nurturing tenderness were 'appropriately' exercised in the home, leaving competition, military struggle and striving for success to be regarded as masculine activities whose proper scenario was the public sphere.

The great achievement of the European myth is usually held to be liberal democracy, which has been exported to various parts of the world. This in turn is underpinned by the post-Enlightenment rationalist concept of the human subject. But Liberal democracies until this century excluded women from voting. When Simone de Beauvoir wrote, in 1943, the classic *La Deuxième Sexe*, which would provide such stimulus for the second wave of the feminist movement, she was still the 'a-political' woman envisaged by Aristotle, unable to vote.[7] Yet it is rash to unload the blame for the extremes of the rational individualism of post-Enlightenment subjectivity on to one person or cause.[8] This has a far more complex development. One cannot simply blame Cartesian or Lockean disengaged rationalism, or Platonic idealism, the industrial revolution or capitalist economics, the dualistic split between inner and outer self, between body and mind, or spirit. All have played their part. But the one feature common to all of these is that the experience and resources of women as articulated by women themselves have never been incorporated into the narrative. The European hero has been a wanderer – from the days of the Greek hero Odysseus, to the fifteenth-century capitalist conquistador 'discovering' Latin America, to the contemporary director of a large multi-national firm. The price of his wanderings is the sedentary, subservient Penelope who keeps the hearth, with a kind of passive waiting which prohibits her own self-awareness and the growth of her own subjectivity.

Christian theology has played its own part in suppressing the full subjectivity of women, in limiting the participation of women in the social contract to that of motherhood, and of making it almost impossible for women to recover from its damaging views on female sexuality. To the objection that I am identifying Christianity with the European myth, whereas in fact Christianity is a world-wide faith, I would reply that this is precisely the damaging consequence of this myth, that it has managed to dominate and impose its interpretation of the liberating gospel message on to the whole world, and in so doing obscure the crucial contributions to early Christianity both of women and of non-European cultural and ethnic groups.

Thus the *civitas Christiana* established by Constantine and Charlemagne demanded the sacrifice of female subjectivity for the sake of the propagation of the species.[9] Become anonymous in order to gain a place in the socio-symbolic contract, in time and history, guaranteed by paternal authority, with God the Father as ultimate guarantor. What was originally a social need then acquired theological justification through a theology of the indissolubility of monogamous marriage.[10] This in its turn is supported by a mystique of suffering service, a spirituality of mediated subjectivity, in which women acquire identity 'in relation to' (husband, child, father), and holiness through the quality of their care and self-denial. That this is still the case is witnessed to by the Pastoral Letter *Mulieris dignitatem*:

> Motherhood implies from the beginning a special openness to the new person: and this is precisely the women's 'part': in this openness, in conceiving and giving birth to a child, the woman 'discovers herself through a sincere gift of self' . . . Scientific analysis confirms that the very physical constitution of women is naturally disposed to motherhood . . . At the same time this also corresponds to the psycho-physical structure of women . . . Motherhood *is linked to the personal structure of the woman and to the personal dimension of the gift* (italics in original).[11]

It is far from the case that a feminist analysis wishes to underrate the experience of motherhood: what is criticized is, first, the restriction of women's identity to motherhood; secondly, the idealization of motherhood as the pre-eminent way to holiness; thirdly, the linking of motherhood with an essentialist view of female identity; and fourthly, the use of motherhood as social institution to control and dominate the lives of women.

Christian theology has locked a distorted view of female sexuality deep into its symbol system. This is most clearly seen in the discourse of Mary, virgin and mother: although the symbolism of Mary has not *always* functioned in an oppressive way for women – for example, in mediaeval times she was a vibrant reminder of the humanity of Jesus, and she clearly has a liberating function in Latin American liberation theology,[12] yet because she is extolled even to the level of 'the feminine dimension of God',[13] and this because of the unique combination of virginal motherhood, she is an icon impossible for ordinary women to follow: moreover, given the popularity of the doctrine of the virgin birth, it is difficult for ordinary married women to come to any healthy view of sexual pleasure, of female 'jouissance'. Although Christianity has constantly condemned the pornographic exploitation of women in its many forms, yet its symbols preserve the dualistic split between the holiness of the Spirit and the unearthly, and the corruptibility and degradation of the body, symbolized by the pornographic female body. It has refused to make the connection between the structures of patriarchal control over women through monogamous marriage and the family, and the encouragement of domestic violence and abuse within it.

Finally, Europe has shown its contempt for the female body preeminently through the Great European witch-craze of the late fifteenth century. It could be said that this is the most overwhelming expression of 'Europe as a sexist myth'. Estimates vary as to how many women were burnt, from 300,000 to several million. The point which needs stressing is that those most victimized were the women who deviated from the sacrificial symbolism of the social contract – motherhood, biological or spiritual – by being unmarried or widowed. As a scholar as recently as 1972 put it:

> . . . we can concede that the small trials may indeed have served a function, delineating the social thresholds of eccentricity tolerable to society, and registering fear of a socially indigestible group, unmarried women . . . Until single women found a more comfortable place in the concepts and communities of Western men, one could argue that they were a socially disruptive element, at least when they lived without family and patriarchal control. In this restricted sense the small witch trial may have even been *therapeutic* . . .[14]

But what can we salvage from Europe's past? Must women be content with being written out of history?

## 2. Reclaiming our story

I will now look at the European 'seamless garment' with a hermeneutic of suspicion which has five elements. First, Europeans are not the élite of Christianity: the blossoming of faith is certainly coming from other parts of the world today, and feminist theology has committed itself to solidarity with the most oppressed of the world, specifically to the eradication of the interlocking oppressions of sexism, racism and the structures of poverty. The sexism of the European myth has prevented white European women from discovering their own racism and collusion in oppressing women from other parts of the world. In fact the current debate on the future of a strengthened Europe presents the real danger that Europe re-forms around exactly the same centre, enacting a new form of the older, sexist myth. The experience of many East European women in the wake of many 'liberation' movements is witness to this: many feel they are still wandering the desert of poverty, of lost ideals, and with no outlook on a Promised Land.

Secondly, there never has been a European 'seamless garment' – rather, a variegated 'coat of many colours'. It is another 'myth' that European culture is represented solely by the art of Michelangelo and Rembrandt, the music of Mozart, the architecture of the Gothic cathedral and the plays of Shakespeare. There has always been a profusion of multi-cultural richness in Europe's midst: even before the Roman army brought North Africans to Britain, the Celtic cultures – whose origins were Mongolian – were enshrining their creative gifts in stone and story in many parts of Europe. There have always been women trying to express themselves in art and poetry. I imagine, too, that there were many Héloises, trying to acquire a theological education in the shadow of the great masters.

Yet the domination of the Christian story and ethic has obscured other faith communities and cultures within Europe's midst, crushing Jew and 'infidel' alike with fire and sword. The ultimate tragic intolerance of another faith story is, of course, the Holocaust.

The third element of a hermeneutic of suspicion with regard to the sexist myth of Europe springs from the damage and exploitation inflicted on many parts of the earth to fill the treasuries of Europe, and to ensure the continuance of a consumptive life-style. This relates directly with the exclusion of women from the formative ethic. For European patriarchal monotheism flourished at the expense of the suppression of the older goddess religions of Greece, Rome and the Celtic deities. With these vanished a sense of respect and reverence for the presence of the divine in the rhythms of the earth, as a *central* value for Christianity (although this has survived in folk religion, in devotions to Mary queen of creation, and in certain mystical writings). The present crisis demands a willingness to listen to the goddess movements, to learn what they teach us about non-exploitative life-styles and sustainable levels of consumption.

And so, fourthly, the only way to uncover another story to live by is to track the roots of the sexist myth to its source: *tracking the roots of the sexist myth to its source is an act of feminist liberation*. It is also a theological activity, rooted in faith in a divinity in love with all creation, particularly with those who are the most oppressed.

'Till we have faces' expresses hope in the justice of the kingdom of God,[15] hope that women will acquire visibility as full human subjects, and not serve merely to be mirrors for the post-Enlightenment super-individual. It recalls one of Europe's foundational stories – the myth of Eros and Psyche. Psyche was not allowed to look on the face of Eros, her husband. Because she yielded to temptation she was condemned to wandering grief-stricken in search of Eros, compelled to fulfill the most dreadful tasks. They were only allowed to behold each other in full mutuality when each had accomplished a journey to maturity. For Christian theology this means that 'psyche' ('soul'), in traditional Augustinian theology more accurately represented by men (and imagined as totally a-physical and a-sexual), must discover a new integrating relationship with Eros. Christian agapé must embrace mutuality. Just as Psyche was joyously re-united with Eros, the Christian psyche-soul can re-discover a sense of God-given embodiment, of being 'earthed' in an elemental energy which is the grace of creation. If Psyche and Eros are re-envisioned, then perhaps there is hope that Europe will discover a new 'logos' other than the 'logos' of the founding European myth. If 'logos' is again to be the divine living Word of communication in mutuality, then it will not be defined in opposition to affectivity and emotion, or limited to an over-rational, objective analysis. It would become a 'listening' logos, which understood its very roots to spring from listening, and from 'hearing into speech'.[16] Only then could Europe discover an alternative logic to that of retaliation, control and dominance.

And so, finally, the task is to re-claim other memories, re-claiming myth in its truest sense as a foundational story. But this time tradition is being challenged and re-membered by those without face or voice in the dominant strand of history, who seek sustaining memories beneath and beyond the dominant sexist myth; who seek to keep faith in a vision of Christian freedom far more radical than the liberalism of the democracies which are the hollow triumph of the sexist myth of Europe.

## Notes

1. Tacitus, *The Annals of Imperial Rome*, London 1956, 258.
2. Eusebius, *Vita Constantini* (F. Winkelmann, Eusebius' Werke $1.1^2$), G.C.2, 1975, 1.27ff.
3. For a re-telling of the Cassandra story, see Christa Wolf, *Cassandra*, London 1984.
4. Peter Brown, *The Body and Society: Men, Women and Sexual Renunciation*, New York and London 1988, xvi–xvii.
5. Virginia Woolf, *A Room of One's Own*, London 1977, 28–36.
6. Virginia Woolf, *Three Guineas*, New York 1938, 109.
7. Simone de Beauvoir, *The Second Sex* (Paris 1943), London 1972.
8. For a careful, reflective analysis of all the influences contributing to the modern sense of self, see Charles Taylor, *Sources of the Self*, Cambridge 1989.
9. For the theme of female sacrificed subjectivity, see Julia Kristeva, *Women's Time*,

in *The Kristeva Reader*, ed. Toril Moi, Oxford 1986, 187–213; also *About Chinese Women*, in ibid., 138–59.

10. The problems of monogamy in Christian theology are well-discussed by Susan Dowell, *They Two Shall Be One: Monogamy in History and Religion*, London 1990.

11. *Mulieris Dignitatem*, Apostolic Letter of Pope John Paul II, London, Catholic Truth Society 1988, 68–9.

12. See I. Gebara and M. C. Bingemer, *Mary, Mother of God: Mother of the Poor*, Maryknoll 1989.

13. See Leonardo Boff, *The Maternal Face of God: The Feminine And its Religious Expressions*, London 1989.

14. H. C. Erik Midelfort, *Witchhunting in South Western Germany, 1562–1684: The Social and Intellectual Foundations*, Stanford 1972, 3.

15. *Till We Have Faces: a Myth Retold*, is actually the title of C. S. Lewis's re-telling of the Psyche-Eros story, London 1956.

16. For an attempt to discover another interpretation of logos within European history, see Andrea Nye, *Words of Power: A Feminist Reading of the History of Logic*, New York and London 1990; Gemma Corradi Fiumara, *The Other Side of Language: A Philosophy of Listening*, New York and London 1990.

# The Christian West – Farewell to an Epoch-Making Vision

## Ottmar John

### 1. The method of theological reflection on Europe

It is evident that the self-awareness of Europeans cannot be the sole basis for a theological understanding of Europe. The catholicity of the church and the universal significance of salvation history preclude theology from relying solely on a European identity, no matter what the shape of that identity may be. Theologically, Europe cannot just be understood in terms of itself. Theologically, it is impossible for Europeans just by themselves to know what Europe really is. For that, what is needed is what Johann Baptist Metz has called the 'view of the others'.

The informative and unavoidable authorities for a theological understanding of Europe are the victims of European history generally, and above all the victims of its efforts at universalization through colonization and imperialism. The information that they provide, their experiences as preserved in recollections, are indispensable testimonies for any verdict on the position of Europe in salvation history (what else would a theology of Europe be?).

This principle of any theology of Europe must now be established and explained in a specific way with a view to learning about Europe and understanding the present, but not, as might seem more obvious at first sight, in a discussion with the testimonies of Latin America, Africa and Asia. Rather, what we must do is to raise the question of the 'awareness of the perpetrators': i.e. the actual experience of the victims matched by an awareness of the subjects who hold and have held power in history and of the way in which their actions shape and have shaped history. What does the reflection of Europeans upon themselves and their history look like?

What theological judgment must be passed on it and what theological criticism made of it?

Because of the complexity of this European thinking about Europe, it is necessary to reduce it in three ways. 1. This account will begin primarily from the discussion in Germany. 2. The historical retrospect will concentrate on that thinking about Europe in which the history of Christian faith is entangled more or less directly: the principle of the authority of the others and of the victims of Europe for an appropriate understanding of Europe will be used in a critical theological discussion of the vision of a Christian West. 3. It is impossible to give an exhaustive description even of this rich vision of the West in terms of the history of ideas; the account must be limited to a rough sketch in which only the systematic essentials of this type of thinking about Europe will be spelt out.

## 2. The idea of 'the West', considered in the light of the 'end of the West'

### (a) A sketch

The idea of 'the West' has both a descriptive and a normative dimension:

1. In nineteenth century historiography 'the West' is one name among many for what is nowadays called the Middle Ages. Granted, it is more original than 'Middle Ages' as the designation of an epoch, but it proved unable to establish itself. There is too much of the mediaeval self-understanding in this designation.[1]

2. From the beginning, the attempts of Catholicism in the nineteenth century to find a political hearing in the rising nation states and in the face of the social question went with an understanding of history for which 'the West' was a normative factor. This was a theme of lay Catholicism,[2] the beginnings of which we may put cautiously with Görres and Romanticism. The discussion of Spengler's pessimistic thesis of the decline of the West is a culmination of this thought. This fear of the final disappearance of the West, shared in part by Catholicism, was countered even before the National Socialist catastrophe by a series of attempts at restoration and rescue. In the face of spiritless technological and economic thinking the aim was to restore and rescue that unity of politics and religion which people thought that they could see achieved in the mediaeval *corpus Christianum*.[3] The effects of this attempt reach right down to the conservative resistance to National Socialism (Schneider and others) and/or into the Adenauer era of the 1950s.

### (b) The following reflections will concentrate on the normative politically

effective dimension of this thought (we need not consider here whether its definitions and distinctions are productive for historical study). The idea of 'the West' in this sense has come to an end in two ways: to a *de facto* end in the beginning of European integration, which consisted in the foundation of the EEC, and a moral end in the Nazi period (for the moral end see the next section).

Remarkably enough, the idea of 'the West' came to an end at the very moment in which Europe became a reality. First, the realities in the Europe of the 1950s and 1960s indicate the end of an awareness which hitherto had been only a vision, an idea, a spirit. Secondly, in the foundation of the EEC there became visible and real the beginning of a Europe the substance of which was massively different from the ideas of 'the West'. Faced with the economic and technical thrust towards development, a thrust which derives its dynamic by abstraction from history and the historical consciousness, the idea of 'the West' in fact loses its function.[4] So the idea of 'the West' is a figure of a historically effective and relevant historical consciousness the normative power of which lies in the past. And this outdated consciousness imagined that it was governed by the past, by the previous era.

Hermeneutically, this suggests that there can be no Christian tradition of the idea of 'the West' without an awareness of the break, of its end. We can understand the idea of 'the West' only if we attempt to make an approach to it through this break, over and above this temporal gap.

*(c)* At heart, the idea of 'the West' was visionary. I claimed above that it lost its function at the time of the largely autonomous economic and technical realization of Europe. Here one amazing fact which needs a good deal of clarification is that such a visionary type of thought vanished almost completely in the face of the realization of something different. In the light of the hermeneutical pointers indicated in *(b)* above, to the effect that this thought can be understood only if one is aware of the break in it, the nature of this farewell to the epoch-making vision of the Christian West sheds light on the content of this vision.

(i)  The idea of 'the West' had little if any analytical value. It was merely a spiritual vision, without an awareness of the difference between vision and reality. It was free-floating – otherwise the dreaming and the fantasizing would hardly have been abandoned so quickly in the face of a substantive realization of another kind.

(ii)  The idea of 'the West' was a backward-looking vision. The content of this vision is the transfiguring and idealizing estimation of mediaeval social and political structures. It was no coincidence that Charlemagne was the historical figure who was often depicted and recalled. If there is anything to be said for describing National Socialism as an impulse towards modernization,[5] it can be concluded that after the Nazi regime and in the time of the economic boom in Germany the power of past eras was finally broken. Only now did it become evident how impossible it was to restore mediaeval conditions. So the decline of the idea of 'the West' was in a way intensified; it drew its inspirations, its constitutive element from past eras, and today is itself a thing of the past.

(iii) For West Germany the period of the beginning of European unity was at the same time the period of the stabilization of a democratic social order and the guarantee of economic development to a hitherto unprecedented degree. Possibly the vision of the West was a 'crisis phenomenon'.[6] It could last as long as the bourgeois society had not yet completely established itself. In the case of Germany – with reference to another Fascist theory, that of the 'nation which arrived late on the scene' (Plessner et al.) – one can claim that the bourgeois revolution had only progressed beyond any question of crisis after the Second World War.[7]

## 3. The idea of 'the West' as substitute nationalism

(a) I have already referred above to the origin of the idea of 'the West' in the nineteenth century. The idea of 'the West' was a kind of basic doctrine of the foreign policy of the Centre Party. This party with its Catholic orientation was the product of the crisis-torn development of the church and Catholicism in the great revolutions of the nineteenth century. The basic problem of the Centre Party now lay in the integration of the Catholic minorities in the population into a Prussian society dominated by a bourgeois Protestantism, without giving up essentials of its own religious and social identity.

One of these essentials was Ultramontanism. One belonged to the church only if one subjected oneself to the Roman pope, not only in fundamental questions of faith and morals but down to many details of the shaping of cultural and political life. And if we remember that the nineteenth century was pre-eminently the century of the nation states and budding nationalism (which in Germany in particular, coming late on the scene, had para-religious or surrogate religious features – Durkheim), we can get some idea of the degree of disintegration in the Catholic population.

In principle, the function of the idea of 'the West' in this aporetic situation can now be interpreted in two ways: 1. As a counterpart to nationalism; accordingly the Christian idea of 'the West' criticized the nation state which set itself up as an absolute. 2. As a substitute concept, as a desperate solution for the Catholics of the German Reich; accordingly this thought was intended to reconcile the tremendous nationalistic emotions bound up with the nation state and Ultramontanism.

The thoroughly defensive way in which the Catholics and the Centre Party carried on their dispute with the Prussian state tells against the first interpretation. So does the introduction of the West as a geopolitical entity, as opposed to the church as an institutional and social entity. A criticism of nationalism would have been a much more natural issue for the church and its characterizing of Catholicism.[8] From this it can be concluded that the anti-nationalistic implications of the idea of 'the West' did not become explicit or dominant; rather, it had a kind of structural affinity to nationalism.

(b) The comments made by Walter Dirks[9] and Reinhold Schneider[10] could be interpreted in this sense. Schneider was possibly the last great intellectual advocate of the vision of a Christian West. However, this lost its worth and its authenticity in the whirlpool of events during the Nazi domination because its foundation and presuppositions disappeared.[11] Although the political forces which went with this self-understanding of the idea of 'the West' were bloodily persecuted by a most aggressive and brutal version of nationalism in the form of National Socialism, the conception of 'the West' had lost its innocence.[12] A rigorous examination of the most recent German past had laid open the ideological function of this vision. An idea which offers so little opposition to ideological instrumentalization is untrue for that reason alone.

To see the idea of 'the West' thus entangled, say, in the crimes of the Third Reich implies a view of Fascist rule as a totality tending towards negativity. Fascism could not be fought with inherited ideas. Those who contented themselves with ideological means of opposing National Socialism and engaged in a purely intellectual conflict themselves incurred guilt. And those who by retreating into privacy or by so-called migration inwards attempted to avoid the complex of guilt, contributed even more to the universalizing and stabilizing of this rule.

To this degree there is not only an actual end to the visions of the West through the realization of Europe, but also a moral end because of its character as a substitute for nationalism or because of its failure to resist being used as an instrument.

## 5. The vision of the West as a 'go East' ideology?

Faber in particular pointed out the ideological character of the idea of the West. With particular reference to Carl Schmitt (who of course hardly spoke explicitly of the West but drew on the arsenal of motives connected with the idea of the West) he argued that the West had been promoted to an ideology of greater space and domination, to a 'militant concept'.[13]

According to Faber's description and evaluation of the idea of the West as a militant concept, 'the West' is not only a political concept with an ideological function but an ideology in itself. For the substance of this notion is made up of a friend-foe scheme and expansionism, the attitudes of world power and subjection. To describe something as 'the West' – as Faber demonstrates with a wealth of references and quotations – means to understand what is thus described as being in opposition to other peoples and cultures.

(b)  It also becomes clear from Faber's study that the focus of this ideology of expansion is predominantly eastwards. In this respect the idea of the West differs from nationalism. The expansionism, the aggressiveness of nationalism is directed against everyone else, geographically speaking in all directions. German nationalism was both anti-Gallic and anti-Slav. But the idea of the West could only turn eastwards. Above all the impossibility of Germany's having an anti-French idea of 'the West', the appearance of the idea in all the Western European countries (Spain, France, England, Austria and the United States – to mention only the most important) and its interchangeability with USA ideologies of expansion,[14] make it clear that the West is aiming single-mindedly at the East.

Now if we investigate the reasons for this expansionism of the idea of the West as demonstrated by Faber, we have to take into account this historical origin of the concept of the West. Its roots possibly reach into the processes of division which became historically definitive in the great schism between East and West in 1054. The great schism marked the end of the unity of Christianity.[15] In this commemorative perspective 'the West' is the designation of a partial sphere of life; those aware of living in the West knew implicitly that they lacked the totality.[16] By its inner logic the idea of the West exerted pressure towards regaining the whole, towards reunion with the East.

And this regaining of wholeness came about historically almost exclusively by way of aggression. Reconquest was its more or less exclusive mode.[17]

(c)  Is not this gaze eastwards an important indication of the continuity of the idea of 'the West' down to the present? I mentioned above the break, the end of the vision of the West, but in the Cold War and in all the various East-West confrontations elements of the idea of 'the West' seem to have been conserved. And particularly in a Christian and a church context, criticism of Eastern socialist societies concentrated on their atheisms, on their hostility to the faith. This criticism also always implied a claim to re-Christianization and re-evangelization. May there not have been a functional identification of Orthodox, schismatic Christianity and Communism here? Was this idea of the West possibly not only used as an ideology against Communism but also as a kind of ideal cause of anti-Communism generally? Because Communism first established itself in the East, in Russia and its satellite states, it fell under the same verdict as Orthodox Christianity. Does the 'go-East' mentality of Western thought reproduce itself in anti-Communism?

Such an interlinking of anti-Communism and the idea of the West means allowing the ideologies and mentalities which may have grown up over centuries through the influence of religion to have a decisive influence on the processes of world history. To speak in this sense of the ideological character of Western thinking *per se* and to identify it as a main cause for expansion eastwards is rather like positing an idealistic concept of ideology and supposing it to be meaningful. Such a question at least relativizes Faber's judgment.

## 6. The controversy over Europe in the theology of history

(*a*) Europe for the first time became the object of specifically theological reflection with Przywara and the brothers H. and K. Rahner. Two basic concepts of post-scholastic theology were normative both for the possibility of a theological understanding of Europe generally and for the tendency of its content: 1. salvation history and 2. humankind as singular.

(i) The basic concept of salvation history is developed from a specific understanding of revelation: revelation is not merely a *locutio Dei*, an expression of the eternal word which always remains the same, in which God communicates something about himself or provides information about himself. Revelation is the action of God communicating himself to human beings and in history. Salvation is history and has a history for us. And so if in theological terms it is necessary to speak of a salvation history, it must be possible to subordinate the various phases of secular history to it.

Both Przywara and Rahner look back at the end of the West. If for Schneider and Dirks, with the awareness of 'the West' a particular *motive* for political action has lost its innocence, Przywara sees in the destruction which the Second World War brought with it a shattering of the West as a secular and sacral 'precinct' of God.[18] At another point he goes still further: 'the West' is not only the sphere in which God's historical action becomes effective but is the 'instrument' of divine action.

Przywara's thesis of the end of the West and the rise of the idea of Europe can thus be understood as the assimilation of the catastrophe of National Socialism into a theology of history. For him, National Socialism was the historically logical result of the secularization of the divine in the self-apotheosis of human beings. However, the result of the war was not that this form of secularization dispensed itself and confirmed the right of both Christianity and the West to exist; rather, its historical result is the *dispersion* of Christians,[19] the Diaspora of world Christianity.[20]

However, Przywara does not just see the end of the West in negative terms; its end is also the liberation of Christianity from its European particularity. The end of the West opens up a visionary perspective on world Christianity. And this dawn of a concrete universality of Christianity has a compelling character because from the beginning humankind was one. In other words, the unity of human beings among themselves[21] is grounded in the singularity of humankind, ultimately in monogenism, which Rahner defends against all modern barriers to understanding and against Darwinism. Because Christians are bound to this truth of faith, that they are descended from just one human couple, they must recognize all human beings in their cultural and also their religious multiplicity.[22] Monogenism proves itself in the view that incarnation does not first come about with the gospel, the Western mode of its realization. Not only, say, the life of the Indians alienated from their culture and incorporated into European Christianity through baptism, but Western military and missionary expansion, encountered people and sinned by them because the Europeans were bound up with them in an original unity.

However, this assumption of the unity of humankind prohibits any sense of superiority and any metaphysical feeling of the greater worth of Europe as compared with other continents. That is a further argument for the need to understand the historical phase of the West and Western culture for theological reasons as being transitory. To go on holding on to the West as a universal and historically final form and to declare this binding would be to go against the tendency of salvation history. The West was and is the final 'instrument of God's infinite love'.[23]

To hold on to its dominance would mean exalting the instrument above its user. According to Rahner and Przywara the West, with its eschatological implications of sunset (German *Abendland*, 'evening land'), was a gigantic misunderstanding. In their ultimately optimistic theology of history, anything but the night follows the evening. It is evident to them that what was first understood as evening was at best afternoon. Theologically, too, 'Middle Ages' is the more appropriate designation.

(b) Whereas Przywara completes the farewell to the West in interpreting the Nazi catastrophe in terms of the theology of history, at the end of this epoch in world history Rahner understands the domination of Europe and the West in the light of his theology of death.[24] Because human beings can never be understood in a theological anthropology as isolated individuals, but in such an anthropology sociality is always constitutive of their being, according to Rahner in the last resort the end of the West can be understood as 'death'. To speak of the death of Europe is then not just metaphor but a concept from the theology of history.

Although this transference of the understanding of death gained from individual biography and its application to the epoch-making macro-sociality of Europe is made a specific issue by Rahner, who reflects on it and produces convincing arguments from his anthropology,[25] it nevertheless causes ambivalence and obscurity. On the one hand, by extending this concept of death Rahner can comprehend historical downfalls and epoch-making revolutions and take them seriously in theological terms. On the other hand the understanding of what happens in dying and death becomes vague: in individual death human beings are redeemed from their particularity and finitude into an actual non-individual omnipresence. By contrast, in its death the West is freed from its false universal claims for a particularity and finitude which are appropriate to reality. For individual human beings, death is the loss of physical and empirical presence, but after its death Europe remains an entity which can be experienced in history and culture. This European culture in its inner multiplicity is released to its distinctiveness and peculiarity only as a result of the death of European world rule. And parallel to the death of the secular world rule of Europe, in the *ars moriendi*, the possibility of the death of the exclusive Western form of Christianity, the true salvation-historical 'value' of the West is revealed.

There is a death of the cultural exlusiveness, the dominance, the absoluteness of the Western spirit. This is liberated from its self-hypostasis to what it really always already was: an instrument (Przywara) which is Western and not all-embracing; it is not a unity of 'morning' and 'evening'. And so it can be concluded that such a liberation to a relative and metaphysically adequate self-assessment, i.e. to a recognition of one's own limitation and finitude, is conversion.

The death of Europe brings about its conversion to liberated finitude, so that Europe takes its place in the manifold community of peoples, cultures, geographical regions and religions. It thus becomes clear that Rahner's talk of the death of Europe is to a considerable degree a criticism of Europe. What in a secular understanding is diagnosed as dying, namely the age of Western European domination of the world, is seen theologically as the self-hypostasis of an era of history which needs to be overcome – and thus the death of Europe is affirmed.

(*c*) At present this critique is made in two models, in two patterns of argument:

(i)  There is a specific present figure of the self-absolutizing of Europe, a form of forgetfulness of its own relativity: that is the merely technical and economic, the secular, Europeanization of the world. J. B. Metz in particular has drawn attention to this connection.[26] A cultural multiplicity or the awareness of a multiplicity of the one humankind which is worth preserving is in fact threatened by the universalizing of a model of society which owes itself above all to nineteenth-century Europe. This universalization is as real a process as European union. It goes on without anyone having to want it; it goes on without ideological disguise and deception. In fact it establishes itself everywhere without having to disarm its victims with false promises and by raising false hopes. Because it has no self-awareness, no spirit, it seems to be anything but universal – the process of the secular Europeanizing of the world is *merely* technical. But precisely because it needs no spirit, precisely because it in fact takes place unconsciously, this process shows its *de facto* universality.

Theology *must* criticize this process of a secular Europeanizing of the world because it offends against the claims of the specifically Christian understanding of the unity of humankind. The unity which comes about as a result of secular Europeanizing is a uniformity, an annihilation or at least a relativization of cultural and religious multiplicity, so that at best it is reduced to the category of folk-lore.[27]

(ii)  If the criticism levelled by political theology conceals the *de facto* universality or totality of secular Europeanizing and derives it from the lack of ideology in this Europeanizing and its uncritical approach, on the other hand there is a mindless negation of Europe: the longing for foreign peoples and cultures and the romanticizing of their situation, their history and their forces is sometimes accompanied by the attempt to blot out Europe completely from their minds and to overlook its *de facto* power by refusing to perceive it. Such a negation of Europe differs from criticism by effectively affirming history. There is and should be Europe – its history of guilt and also its capacity for self-criticism are an abiding legacy without which there is no unity of humankind.

(*d*)  To what degree does the critical theological discussion of the vision of a Christian West and the idea of its end lead to the theological *a priori* of any understanding of Europe, to the eyes of the others, to the recognition of the authority of Europe's victims for its understanding of itself? A critical analysis of the concept of the West and an identification of its theologically relevant content could show that it contains the consciousness of finitude and relativity – however covered over and hidden, however misunderstood and ideologically misused. Those who called its sphere, its land, 'the West' knew that with it they owed themselves to an event outside themselves. Thus e.g. for Hugo Rahner the West is the land on which the shadow of the cross falls at the rising of the sun.[28]

To this extent there is a need to criticize the salvation-historical parallelizing of the West with Israel in both Karl Rahner and in Erich Przywara. For them, the West was a similar phase of salvation history to Israel. Both are things of the past and an abiding heritage.[29]

Is the rising sun, the morning for the West, the same as the West for the one world? In connection with the saving event the West can be described as the place and time in which it did not take place: both the East and the one world differ from it – to both, what took place almost 2000 years before on the soil of Israel is an inward matter.

(*e*)  Finally, we should once again recall the significance of the West as a temporal metaphor. For Karl Rahner, the self-understanding of part of the earth as 'the West' seemed to be the simple error of an eschatology with a false identification and termination. In its place he sketches out a theological concept of Europe in which Western Christianity on the one side and Eastern Christianity on the other can again be considered together and in their relationship to one another, and in which Europe comes into its own in its particularity, in the death of its false absoluteness. The end of false absoluteness now leads, as I have shown above, to a criticism of secular Europeanizing; if, however, with Metz we note that here we have a largely autonomous material process, it becomes clear that Rahner's critical talk of the death of Europe is less the description of an already real state than the basis of challenges to political and moral action.

For Przywara, the shattering of the West by National Socialism at least also had a productive function: the shock of the Second World War and its devastations taught people to see that the end of history has not been reached with the end of the pre-eminence of the West. History goes on, and after the Second World War is replaced by the rivalry between the Soviet Union and the USA. Against Przywara we must now ask whether the conception of the Nazi catastrophe as a catharsis which has freed Catholics from false thought, from a fixation on the past, is theologically appropriate. Can a crime be productive in salvation history?

The obvious difficulties over both the two theological positions on the end of the West which I have indicated here can possibly be removed by a critical inversion of the concept of the West. Here we should cautiously assert that the eschatological misunderstanding of which Rahner and Przywara accuse the concept of the West is at least an analytically productive misunderstanding: to diagnose the end of the West without affirming this state as either neutral or positive for salvation history can lead to important diagnostic insights into the prevailing tendencies in development. These are fundamentally different from interest in a dull and unimaginative restoration. Insight into the end of the Western era can arouse interest in disclosing the hidden negativity of the victorious forces. Hermeneutically, who would rather be in a position of seeing behind the splendour of the new world age, postmodernity, world civilization or whatever other name is given to it, the reality of oppression and hunger, exploitation and economic concentration? Those who are subject to the historical process can at the moment of realistic insight into their defeat attain a high sensitivity to the situation of the marginalization of the majority of the world's population. The historical moment of downfall is at the same time that of conversion. As Rahner says, a West which has come to an end is something qualitatively quite different for salvation history from one which tries to repristinate its former misunderstanding of itself in self-hypostasis.

A retrospect on the end of the West rests on an awareness of a present at the centre of which stands the time-critical predicate of night. Such a way of thinking raises the question (something that is historically obsolete can still raise questions: the verdicts are spoken by those who have survived it) whether the many situations of suffering in the world do not call for a theology of night. A theology of night could take up those mystical experiences and traditions in which it is possible to detect the combination of night and experiences of suffering on the one hand and the hope for the light which is heightened in it. To link up with this, however, would mean to articulate mystical experiences which are closely attached to society and empirically transparent. Perhaps a theology of the night, such a critical inversion of the Christian idea of the West, could take in the truth of those texts in which various Jewish survivors of the Holocaust recall the cruelty of our most recent history, to which they have attached that word which denotes the time which has already followed in the West.[30]

*Translated by John Bowden*

## Notes

1. The clear verdict on the unusability and historical vagueness of the concept of 'the West' can be interpreted in this way – there are extensive examples in E. Wolf's article 'Abendland', *Die Religion in Geschichte und Gegenwart*[3], Tübingen 1959, Vol. 1.

2. The specifically 'lay character' is evident from the fact that e.g. in 1870 the Curia took a stand against this position: cf. F. Heer, 'Römische Kirche in Europa', in E. Uhl (ed.), *Europa – Herausforderung für die Kirchen*, Frankfurt 1973, 100ff.

3. Cf. C. Schmitt, *Römischer Katholizismus und politische Form*, Munich 1925.

4. This seems to be contradicted by the fact that Schumann, de Gasperi and Adenauer, the fathers of European union after the catastrophe of the Second World War, 1. had in view the union of the West; 2. claimed Christianity, and especially Catholicism as the fundamental rival system to Communism with the dimension of a world-view. Both these aspects seem to indicate a continuity of the political influence of the idea of the West rather than to its end. However, the fact that Western Europe began to form itself into the EEC is not sufficient reason to see the consciousness of being 'the West' as a specifically Catholic view of the world and history having an effect on the rise of the modern world. The substantive anti-Communism of the Adenauer era (in which West Germany was founded and developed) need not necessarily be explained in terms of the influence of Catholic thought. There are also other anti-Communisms and themes opposed to the USSR than the conflict between religion and a state with an atheistic constitution. Rather than assuming that the idea of the West had some influence on the period of West German development and the Cold War, we should take into account that the first great Europeans made use of individual elements of the idea of the West which could in fact have been ideological set pieces and random ideal borrowings from a figure of thought which was already a thing of the past at this time; for more detail cf. ch. 6.

5. Cf. D. Schoenbaum, *Die braune Revolution. Eine Sozialgeschichte des Dritten Reiches*, Munich 1980; R. Dahrendorf, *Gesellschaft und Demokratie in Deutschland*, Munich 1971.

6. Cf. The contribution by Gesine Schwan in P. Haungs (ed.), *Europäisierung Europas? Veröffentlichungen der deutschen Gesellschaft für Politikwissenschaft*, Vol. 6, Baden-Baden 1991.

7. The cross-check for this thesis would be a demonstration that the idea of the West has also been superseded in countries in which the modern period had reached some degree of stability earlier. However, it is impossible to do that in detail here.

8. In nineteenth-century ecclesiology the church was always a relevant counterpart to the state; the neo-scholastic doctrine of the church stressed the visibility of the church, its character as an institution or society.

9. 'The conservative character of the era . . .'

10. R. Schneider, *Macht und Gnade. Gestalten, Bilder und Werte in der Weltgeschichte*, Leipzig 1940, 167f., 'a veiled day'.

11. 'Fathers and grandfathers have slowly become remote from belief', ibid., 81.

12. See ibid., 77.

13. Cf. R. Faber, *Abendland. Ein Kampfbegriff*, Hildesheim 1979, 201.

14. 'Euroamerica', or 'Atlantis'; see Faber, *Abendland* (n. 13), 91–107; similarly for Brazil A. Moreira, '. . . *doch die Armen werden das Land besitzen' (Ps. 37.11). Eine theologische Lektüre der Landkonflikte in Brasilien*, Mettingen 1990, 266f., with reference to Schmitt, and 274ff., with reference to the 'ideology of national security' in

Latin American military dictatorships, which he interprets as a reception of Schmitt's 'principle of greater space'.

15. In another context J. Verweyen, *Gottes letztes Wort*, Düsseldorf 1991, 218–20, has referred to the traumatic significance of the Western scheme and the way in which it irritates identity, and also to the significance of the loss of the mediation of salvation within the world which was clearly guaranteed in the papacy.

16. As Karl Rahner puts it, the West has to transcend itself, in principle to surpass itself, as a factor in salvation history: 'Abendland', *Herders Theologisches Taschenbuchlexikon* 1, 22.

17. This may be why Rahner speaks of a transcending of the West 'in guilt' and says that after the 'dropping of Byzantium as a counterpart, of the West increasingly only Europe is left' (ibid.).

18. E. Przywara, *Logos. Logos-Abendland-Reich-Commercium*, Düsseldorf 1964, 100.

19. Ibid.

20. Ibid., 101.

21. *Lumen Gentium*, 1.

22. Monogenism implies that human difference derives from 'begetting', not multiple 'settlement'. In other words, monogenism implies unity of species. K. Rahner, 'Theological Reflexions on Monogenism', *Theological Investigations* 1, London and New York 1961, 229–96: 289. This 'unity of the human race' is not 'seen merely in the one transcendent divine origin', but in 'the real unity of origin and unity of order of the material world', ibid., 294.

23. Przywara, *Logos* (n. 18), 101.

24. See K. Rahner, 'Die Frage nach der Zukunft Europas', in *Schriften zur Theologie* XVI, 66ff., 85.

25. Ibid., 69.

26. Cf. e.g. F. X. Kaufmann and J. B. Metz, *Zukunftsfähigkeit. Suchbewegungen im Christentum*, Freiburg 1987, 138.

27. Here a structural parallelism is evident between the idea of the West and Metz's ecclesiological thesis of the cultural polycentrism of the world church: if the Catholic idea of the West was at least also an attempt on the part of Catholicism to resist nationalism successfully, Metz's polycentrism is the profound Europeanization of the world.

28. Cf. H. Rahner, *Abendland*, Freiburg, Basel and Vienna 1966, 6.

29. Cf. K. Rahner, 'Die Frage nach der Zukunft Europas' (n. 24), 72, 74; Przywara, *Logos* (n. 18).

30. E.g. Elie Wiesel and Edgar Hilsenrath.

# II · Challenge

# 'The Rich Keep Getting Richer'–Economic Justice for All

## Wolfgang Kessler

### 1. Holes in the cloak of silence

It has long been known that the rich of the world keep getting richer and owe a considerable part of their prosperity to the poverty in the so-called 'Third World'. However, so far the discussions about the injustice of the world economic order have taken place exclusively in small circles. There is one basic reason for this: people in the prosperous world have not been affected by the injustices of the world economy. So at first the topic did not appear even in political discussion. What politicians answer questions which are not put to them by the voters? In this way people in the rich industrial countries have been able to repress their responsibility for the poverty in the other two-thirds of the world under a cloak of silence.

Now, however, the situation is beginning to change, and holes are appearing in the cloak of silence. An increasing number of people in the First World are becoming aware that the destruction of the rain forests also has a detrimental effect on the environment in their part of the world as a result of changes in the climate. Nor is that all. After decades in which the industrialized countries have refused people in the southern half of the world their share of prosperity, now the latter are seeking it themselves. The number of refugees driven by poverty is increasing, and with it an anxiety that the prosperous part of the world will lose its prosperity. The governments of the industrial countries are still restricting themselves to keeping out refugees – to the point where an iron curtain has been built by the USA in order to protect its border against Mexican immigrants. The governments have still to take account of the real causes of the world-wide refugee movement, and for a long period they have refused to join in any open discussion of the structural problems of the world economy which for decades have led to the rich constantly getting richer and the poor constantly getting poorer.

## 2.  The structural problems of the world economy

### (a)  The falling price of raw materials

Since the colonial period, the developing countries have suffered from a very one-sided production structure imposed on them by the industrial countries. The colonists destroyed the widespread self-sufficiency in the areas of the so-called Third World that they conquered. In its place they introduced large estates and grew luxury raw materials like coffee and tea to export back home, rather than food for the needs of the local population. The consequences of this colonizing are still evident today. According to information from the United Nations Conference for Trade and Development (UNCTAD), in eighty-four developing countries raw materials still account for more than fifty per cent of exports. Consequently many of these developing countries find themselves in an economic vicious circle: if they want to import machinery, motor vehicles, spare parts or energy for their own industrial development from the industrial countries, they have to pay for the imports with raw materials – if they cannot do this, they either have to do without the imports and therefore lose out on economic development or fill the growing gap in finance with ever higher credits. So it is no coincidence that the foreign debt of many developing countries has risen dramatically, especially over the past decade.

One reason for this is the equally dramatic drop in the price of raw materials. According to the HWWA Institute for Economic Research in Hamburg, the world market prices for the most important raw materials in 1986 were thirty per cent below those of 1980. In the second half of the 1980s this trend intensified still further. Whereas in 1985 92.5 sacks of coffee or 44.3 metric tonnes or bananas were enough to buy a seven- to ten-ton truck from a major German manufacturer, by the end of 1989 the developing countries were already having to pay 332.6 sacks of coffee or 69.4 tonnes of bananas for the same vehicle. The world market has forced the raw material producers into a corner. All in all, the developing countries are having to export increasingly large amounts of raw material to pay their foreign debts, and at the same time the free market is responding to the growing availability of raw materials with rapidly falling prices.

### (b)  The European Community hogs it

While the governments of the rich countries 'innocently' point to market pressures in the raw materials sector, they themselves vigorously intervene in the free market when their vital interests are at stake – for example, in the sphere of agriculture. Although enough food is produced world-wide to feed even a growing world population, more and more of the food is being pre-empted by small minorities of this population: for example, by the European Community. To pile up a gigantic meat mountain annually, the EC uses around 40% of the world's grain, half the world's total fish catch (as fish meal), 60-70% of oil crops and a third of the milk produce of cows, pigs and poultry; 40% of this animal food comes from the Third World. In transforming these enormous amounts of food into meat, the world population is simply using enormous numbers of calories. A hectare of land used for growing soya beans can provide the necessary protein and calories for around 5000 people. If this area is used as pasture, it can feed only 191 people.

And this is far from being the end of the vicious circle. Since the European community is producing too much meat, its farmers are being given subsidies to export their meat at giveaway prices throughout the world. Every year 27 million tonnes of grain, 1.5 million tonnes of meat and around 2 million tons of milk products from the European community flood all over the world. The consequences for the developing countries are catastrophic: 'refined foods' flow into their markets at a price which is beyond the reach of the masses of hungry people, but at the same time still low enough to discourage the local producers and force their products out of the markets. The result is that the satiated minority of the world population keeps getting fatter, while less and less food is left over for the hungry.

## (c)  The end of the road for countries with cheap labour?

We find a similar picture when it comes to industrialization, which is the most important area of economic development. During the 1960s and 1970s a number of countries in the Third World, especially in Asia and Latin America, took the course of industrialization along Western lines. They offered large companies major advantages: low labour costs, low taxation, few conditions imposed by the state and little potential for resistance on the part of the workers by trade union restrictions. Nevertheless, this strategy of 'selling out' to Western big business enabled only a few states to make the jump into the industrial age, the social and political value of which was in any case disputed.

All in all, the Third World plays a completely subordinate role in the world production of industrial goods: according to UNCTAD figures the share of the whole of the Third World in global industrial production was running at around 11% in 1988; that of the whole of black Africa amounted to 0.6%. According to the statistics of the German Federal Ministry for Economic Co-operation, the share of the industrial countries in world exports has risen since 1975 from 65.6% to 70.7%, whereas that of the developing countries has declined from 24.6% to 19.7%. Moreover, even this tiny share of the Third World in world trade and production is in danger. Thus many Third World countries fear that the coming European domestic market will be shut off from the world market, thus reducing the possibilities for exporters from developing countries.

In addition, the strategy of an 'export-orientated industrialization' which many Third World countries are following as a way of riding out the storm will be overtaken by technological developments in the industrial countries. The micro-electronic revolution in production processes is so far advanced that the proportion of labour costs to total costs is constantly dropping, at least in the larger concerns – in heavily rationalized businesses, labour costs are already under 10%. Thus the low labour costs of developing countries are becoming increasingly less significant as motivation for big businesses to invest abroad. This could lead to the realization of the nightmare described by Franz Josef Hinkelammert, an economist from Costa Rica, to a relatively small audience during the German Katholikentag in Berlin in 1990: 'Computers and automation are increasingly making the labour force of the South superfluous. What the excessively powerful North will need in the future will be the seas, certain raw materials for which there is as yet no substitute, and the ecological resources of the Third World. But the people of the South will no longer be needed. So-called intelligent machines in the First World are producing goods at much more favourable prices and with far less errors than low-paid workers in the countries of the Third World.'

### 3. Poverty and foreign debt, or the balance in the development account

For the first time in a long while, in its 1990 report on world developments the World Bank in Washington DC took stock of developments in the world economy over recent decades with inexorable frankness:

Many developing countries have not only failed to keep pace with the industrial countries; in absolute terms their income has actually declined. The standard of living of millions of people in Latin America is now lower than it was at the beginning of the 1970s. In most African countries south of the Sahara the standard of living has sunk to a level which had last been reached in the 1960s. Such facts, unusual as they are, do not yet touch on the desperate situation of the poorest of all, whose hopes have been largely dashed, even if incomes have risen elsewhere in the Third World. For many of the poor of the world, the 1980s were a 'lost decade' – in fact a catastrophe.

The dream of economic development for many Third World countries along the lines of the Western industrial countries has not only proved unrealistic. For many of these countries it has resulted in a life-threatening aftermath in the form of higher foreign debts. These have arisen as a result of a development within the world economy in which the Third World countries have not been able to pay for their expensive imports by exporting cheap raw materials and simple consumer goods. According to information supplied by the World Bank, these foreign debts are now approaching the unimaginable sum of US$1400 billion. This mountain of debt symbolizes the historically-conditioned economic structural defects of the developing countries and their faded dream of economic improvement with the aid of the industrialized countries. The foreign debt is the mathematical proof of an unjust world economic order.

At the same time, this debt contributes to the further enrichment of the rich. Through interest payments, in 1988 alone in excess of $52 billion more flowed from the Third World to creditors in the industrial countries than the total capital which flowed from the rich North to the poor South (through development aid, new credits and foreign investments). In this way foreign debts are bringing about a constant transfer of capital into the rich world.

## 4. The bitter consequences of foreign debt

The consequences of foreign debt are more than bitter for the countries concerned. For the pressure of debt is forcing their governments, even those which are democratically elected and orientated on the needs of their people, to adopt two economic policies: they must export as much as possible and import as much as possible, in order to balance their budgets. However, this increase in exports at any price means that resources which were previously reserved for domestic use are now exported. This is particularly significant in the sphere of food production, where more and more products are grown and produced for export and fewer for home consumption. This makes food in the countries concerned scarce and dear – and thus beyond the reach of broad strata of the population. Moreover, the governments of countries which are deeply in debt often subordinate the whole of their policies to the goal of increasing exports: this means that trees are felled and carted off with no concern for the natural environment, and the state calls for lower and lower wages so that the country's businesses can compete on the world market.

The drastic reduction in income to relieve the pressure on the other side of the budget has equally catastrophic consequences. Development projects come to a halt because there are no spare parts; transport is limited for lack of energy; foodstuffs become scarce because they are no longer imported; medicines run out. Against this background it is becoming clear that the Third World debt crisis is further intensifying the sell-off of economic and social resources by the developing countries to the industrial countries which is taking place anyway within the framework of the world economic order. So far no solution for this problem is in sight, although bankers and politicians have been concerned with it since 1982. Thus far it has proved possible only to slow down the growth of the mountain of debt by various rescheduling mechanisms and regular debt management – nevertheless, year by year the foreign debt of the Third World continues to increase.

## 5.  From North-South dialogue to a monologue by the North

The economic crisis in the Third World has also decisively changed the North-South dialogue to which such great hopes were once attached. In the 1970s the Third World countries confronted the North with the demand for a new world economic order; during the 1980s the industrial countries began their counter-offensive. In the framework of the eighth round of negotiations of the General Agreement on Trades and Tariffs (GATT), the 'Uruguay Round', they wanted to impose basic rules for a world free trade which went far beyond those agreed on by the 105 signatories of GATT when it was first established in 1947. Hitherto it had been a matter of abolishing excise duties, limiting quantities and regulating the quality of merchandise – with the aim of making trade easier world-wide. To the developing countries as the weaker partners this aim was already controversial enough. But in the eighth round, basic rules were discussed to regulate the access of service industries to the markets of the signatory states and basic agreements for foreign investors which were to limit to a minimum the economic and political conditions that could be imposed by the host countries. The General Secretary of GATT, Arthur Dunkel, sees in such agreements a new quality of free trade for the whole world:

If we are talking of liberalization in the area of service industries and restriction on the conditions imposed by states on investments, then we are talking of national laws. We are then intervening in spheres which have hitherto been regarded as spheres of national autonomy. That is the revolutionary aspect of the Uruguay round.[1]

These efforts are revolutionary in two respects. First, the aims of the negotiations show that the industrial countries want the world economy to be one great domestic market in which governments can put very few obstacles in the way of the investment plans of great trans-national concerns without contravening international agreements. From the perspective of the Third World this is a threatening concept, but there is little they could do in the face of the economic offensives of the great corporations. For the Indian GATT representative B. K. Kutshi, who was the Third World's representative and spokesman in the Uruguay round,

> many demands of the industrial countries in the framework of the Uruguay round thus show considerable disregard for the feelings of the Third World. Our concerns about our future development and our needs are just not taken into account. The demands of the industrial countries prove what they want to achieve worldwide through GATT: their global economic dominance.[2]

However, the negotiations within the framework of the Uruguay round are revolutionary for another reason: they symbolize a shift of power in the North-South discussion. For two decades the North-South dialogue has taken place within the framework of the United Nations, above all of UNCTAD. The controversial topics of this dialogue were to become the basic pillars of a new world economic order: more development aid, higher prices for raw materials, a transfer of technology to the Third World and free access of producers from developing countries to the markets of the industrial countries. Although the governments of the North had kept blocking the Third World demands, this shift of the North-South dialogue to GATT is more than a change of curtailment: by concentrating the negotiations on the goal of free world trade the industrial countries have been able to exclude from the discussion themes they do not like and to involve the developing countries in an international obligation to build up free world trade which will be most advantageous to the most competitive economies. In this way the North-South dialogue has become a monologue by the North.

## 6. The opportunity: from Iron Curtain to global social state

Against this background, world society is at present further away than ever from a solution to these urgent problems – even though the problems of the Third World are also affecting the rich industrial countries in the form of environmental destruction and refugees. In this situation it is not surprising that the rich world is primarily dissociating itself from the consequences of its policy. Its reactions extend from the erection of an iron curtain across the USA, through strict regulations about asylum and immigration in the EC, to military scenarios for possible conflicts with 'aggressive Third World governments', as the American Defence Secretary, Dick Cheney, puts it. However, for experts on development like Elmar Altvater, a political scientist at the Free University of Berlin, this policy of dissociation is ultimately an illusion:

> The 'civilization' of capitalism may indeed have some prospects of success in the industrial countries. But the 'civilization' in the rich north is matched by a 'de-civilizing' south of the Mediterranean and the Rio Grande. If we take into account the backlash in the form of the decivilizing of capital in other areas of the world, it is questionable whether a civil and democratic society can be developed and sustained in a fortress, shut off from the rest of the world, which is so much larger.[3]

Those who for decades now have been working for more just economic relations between the industrial countries and the developing countries see in this illusion one great and perhaps last chance for the world. For example, at the Evangelischer Kirchentag in the Ruhr in June 1991, Jan Pronk, for many years the Deputy General Secretary of UNCTAD and now Development Aid Minister for the Netherlands, called for global agreements between the world governments as an answer to the globalization of the problems. In principle, Pronk would like to see the kind of development that took place in the last century in the industrialized countries: under the pressure of social movements liberal economic national states were developed into social states. Pronk is well aware that the development to a world social state is unrealistic under present political conditions. Nevertheless, at present proposals are being discussed which could be the first steps in the direction of a world social state:
— One significant step would be political agreements between producers and consumer countries over higher and more stable prices for raw materials. As this would involve intervention in the free play of market forces, this proposal is particularly unpopular in industrial countries with a market economy. At the same time higher raw material costs would be in

the long-term interests of the whole of world society. First, they would decisively improve the financial situation of many developing countries and redistribute capital from the rich part of the world to the poor part. Secondly, the high raw material prices would stimulate the whole world economy into saving non-renewable raw materials and sparing resources for future generations.

All strategies for improving the economic situation in the Third World call for a controlled reduction of foreign debt: first by writing it off where this is possible, in agreement with the Western banks, and secondly by new forms of recycling these debts which could then even make a contribution to development. One thinks of the idea that the debtor countries should pay part of their foreign debts in national currency into a fund from which projects with a social and ecological orientation could be financed. All in all imagination can range free in working out how to rid the Third World of debt. Just one thing is certain. Unless the developing countries are freed from the strait-jacket of foreign debt, the room for any independent social development within them will be incredibly small.

— The first steps towards a 'world social state' also call for a move away from the sacrosanct principle of free international trade. Free international trade makes no contribution to the social and ecological conditions of the Third World. On the contrary, in the harsh competition for the attractive markets in the industrial countries, on grounds of cost the producers in the Third World are looking for the areas with the worst ecological and social conditions. The alternative to this is a world trade which is socially and ecologically regulated, in which the industrial countries attach minimum ecological and social conditions to imports from the so-called Third World. By this measure it would be possible to kill two birds with one stone: first, social and ecological conditions in the Third World would improve as a result of this external pressure. Secondly, this regulation would put a rein on the worst ecological and social conditions, from which not least the producers in the industrial countries would also profit – to this degree this measure would be a first step towards a social and ecological world economic policy.

Granted, these three basic demands for a juster world social order would only be a small step on the way to a world social state, but in present political conditions they would be a great stride. The celebrations over the victory of capitalism in the competition between systems are still obscuring the fact that the economic and thus also the political future of the world depends on how far a new and juster world economic order can restrain the destructive forces of international capitalism. Here the decisive task will be the establishment of a different lifestyle and economy in the industrial countries, which will manage with a substantially reduced use of raw materials, energy and consumer goods. Only on this basis will the Third World be given the necessary sustainable space for growth in order to raise the standard of living of its own populations without destroying the ecology of the whole world. Only if the rich of the world learn to share can the poor of the world become richer without damage to all. Or in the words of Franz Kamphaus, Bishop of Limburg: 'We must live differently, so that others can live differently.'[4]

*Translated by John Bowden*

### Notes

1. Cf. *epd Entwicklungspolitik* 1/88, 3.
2. Cf. *epd Entwicklungspolitik* 18–18/90, 21.
3. *Frankfurter Rundschau*, 3 July 1991, 16.
4. Quoted in *epd – Dritte Welt-Information* 6/86, 6.

# A New Peace Policy. A System of Collective Security In and For Europe

## Dieter S. Lutz

### 1. The starting point

*(a) The threat*

Looking back on the past decades of East-West confrontation the question of the possible contours of a new peace policy still sounds like a utopian notion, if not a dangerous illusion. But the current changes in the states of the former Warsaw Pact, especially in the Soviet Union, show that when it comes to policies for peace and security, even utopias can become reality.

A series of facts and indicators shows that the new thinking propagated by Soviet Union is meant seriously. This already includes the withdrawal of Soviet forces from Afghanistan and the implementation of considerable advances in unilateral disarmament, including the demobilization of more than half a million soldiers. Domestically, it includes the withdrawal of the republics from the union in a strengthening of their independence, measures and regulations leading to the transition to a market economy, the extension of possibilities for participation in society, the pluralization and democratization of political decisions, and finally the promise of a military withdrawal from border territories to Central Europe. Further-more it includes assent to German reunification and – something that formerly seemed inconceivable – since July 1990 also the integration of the whole of Germany into NATO. Certainly we cannot yet speak of a final and complete 'transformation of the Soviet system', nor may we be able to in the foreseeable future. But the reforms – or better the revolutionary changes – in the Soviet Union are certainly more than merely cosmetic.

However, the changes in the Warsaw Treaty organization are not just limited to the Soviet Union. On the contrary, at the moment the constitutional head of Poland, Lech Walesa, is the leading representative of the former opposition and trade union movement Solidarity; the state president of Czechoslovakia is the writer Vaclav Havel, who was persecuted under Communist rule; the parliamentary president is Alexander Dubcek, the author of the 'Prague spring'. The government of Hungary is headed by the president of the newly-founded liberal-conservative party Hungarian Democratic Forum, Jozsef Antall.

In short, there is no denying the fact that the Communist Eastern block no longer exists as a block and an enemy. Since April 1991, even the Warsaw Pact has ceased to exist as a formal institution. Possibly for a while there will still be political combinations and interests capable of forming a joint military defence against outside attacks from one or more of the former Warsaw Pact states, but this is not to be seen as a threat, any more than a joint aggression by the former Warsaw Pact states seems imaginable in the future. That the former opponents of the pact have themselves come to this conclusion is shown quite clearly in the 'Joint Declaration' of the NATO states in Paris in November 1990. This declaration states, among other things:

The signatories solemnly declare that in the dawn of a new age in European relationships, they are no longer opponents, but will build up new partnerships and extend to one another the hand of friendship.

*(b)  The development of arms control*
This situation is confirmed in fact by the positive assessment of the present threat – at least at first glance – in the development of European disarmament and arms control at the beginning of the 1990s. The following points may be noted:

— the withdrawal of North American chemical weapons from the Federal Republic of Germany;
— the reduction of foreign NATO forces on German territory;
— the widespread disbanding of the former military forces in the German Democratic Republic;
— the commitment to reduce the German Bundeswehr to 370,000 by the end of 1994;
— the agreement to withdraw Soviet troops from Germany by the end of 1994;
— the withdrawal of Soviet troops from Hungary, Poland and Czechoslovakia;
— the conclusion of a partial agreement on 17 November 1990 within the framework of the Conference on Security and Co-operation in Europe, and especially

— the conclusion of the first treaty on 19 November 1990 within the framework of the negotiations on conventional forces in Europe.

At the latest with the beginning of the Vienna negotiations on conventional weapons in March 1989, the NATO countries and the former Warsaw Pact countries accepted the logic of the considerations of joint security and the structural prevention of aggression; it is the aim of these talks further to strengthen stability and security in Europe by the removal of assymetries, and also by disarmament, arms limitation and relocation, and especially by the removal of offensive capabilities. The participants in the talks are the member states of NATO and the Warsaw Pact. The area covered is the territory of all the member countries in Europe, from the Atlantic to the Urals and the Caspian Sea, including all the European islands (the exception is a narrow strip of land in the southeast of Turkey facing Iran, Iraq and Syria). The talks cover conventional land-based forces. Thus the Vienna negotiations cover all the conventional forces of the formerly 23 (including East Germany), now 22 member countries, both within the nations' frontiers and abroad.

A first result of the first round of negotiations was a treaty which was signed on 19 November 1990. It provides for a limitation or a reduction of the potential both of NATO and the Warsaw Pact, within a period of 40 months, to 20,000 tanks, 30,000 armoured vehicle carriers, 20,000 pieces of artillery, 6,800 war planes and 2,000 military helicopters, each graded in four zones. If the reductions on the Western side, including those in the German Bundeswehr, look somewhat modest, at least one can say that deep cuts have been made in the offensive potential of the Warsaw Pact countries. For example, in the case of tanks they amount to almost 50%.

*(c) An analysis of the dangers*

From the arms control developments briefly sketched out above and the processes of change in the former Warsaw Pact organization and the Soviet Union which I have described, can one conclude that fundamental changes in the structure of the international system have already taken place which allow us even now to talk of the final removal of war as an institution and the formation of a permanent and stable order of peace? Doubts are in place here. Despite the Vienna talks, in Eastern and Western Europe at least for the moment there are still tens of thousands of offensive weapons and millions of soldiers under arms. In addition, in recent years research has been carried on into new arms technologies (e.g. in space), and new weapons (e.g. binary gases) have been produced. And despite arms treaties and negotiations the superpowers alone have stationed thousands of new strategic weapons (vertical proliferation); in addition the number of actual or potential nuclear countries is constantly increasing (horizontal proliferation). Moreover the same is also true of the spread of chemical weapons and the possession of ballistic missiles. Furthermore, the arms budget has risen worldwide in more than 60% of countries, and weapons and forces are being used in around forty theatres of war. The most recent instances include the Gulf War (1990/1991). So neither the global arms race nor the danger of wars has been overcome; regional conflicts and, increasingly, ethnic conflicts, along with the inbuilt dynamic of the complex arms race and constantly new military technologies make not only conventional but also nuclear wars conceivable. And these – as I have already stressed – whether deliberately or unintentionally, consciously or by mistake, whether preventive or retaliatory, risk spreading beyond their original limits.

Furthermore peace is more than just a cease-fire. It is also the process by which violence, exploitation, hunger and oppression are done with and the natural foundations of life are preserved or restored. In the Third World millions of people are still dying from hunger and its consequences, resources are getting scarcer, pastureland, meadowland and arable land is being devastated, and wars are being waged. In the long term we cannot exclude the possibility that one of these regional wars may spark off a future world war which even drags in the nuclear superpowers or other European states. But even without the outbreak of a world war, we can no longer deny the global dangers which extend beyond national frontiers and which result from violence in the form of poverty in the Third World: the cutting down of forests in the Third World has far-reaching world-wide consequences for the environment; the misuse of chemicals rebounds on the industrial countries in food and consumer goods from the Third World; the security risks of civil nuclear reactors in the Third World concern everyone.

In particular, as the Brundtland Report points out, 'the ecological crisis, which is becoming increasingly grave, in some circumstances represents a greater threat to national survival than a well-armed neighbour with evil intent or hostile military alliances'. The increasing environmental catastrophes are no longer 'natural' catastrophes in the traditional sense but are the consequences of a wrong policy which extends beyond national frontiers. A world-wide environmental collapse is already on the horizon today: the supplies of drinking water are getting worse, the forests are dying, the protective ozone layer over the earth is disappearing. Acid rain is destroying both plants and marine life; at the same time it is destroying our artistic and architectural heritage. The level of carbon dioxide in the air is increasing. The climate is changing. Soil is deteriorating in quality and being eroded, deserts are expanding. The extinction of species is increasing rapidly. Poisonous chemicals and waste products are leading to almost insoluble problems of disposal, waste management and storage. Nor is that all: even 'environmental wars' cannot be ruled out in the future, whether as wars *against* those who cause (or threaten to cause) environmental catastrophes or as aggression *by means of* weapons which destroy the environment.

Neither science nor politics is expected to overcome the majority of the dangers I have mentioned. New technologies must safeguard the future. But the dangers and risks which in turn are bound up with these technologies or are caused by them, transcending as they do national frontiers, seem to be a considerable obstacle in the way of peace. Space research can open up new dimensions to human beings, but it can also be misused to attain first-strike capabilities. Microelectronics can make workers' lives easier, but they can also make wars seem viable. Information technology can serve towards national and international co-operation, but can also lead to a security state. Gene technology can help to remove diseases and hunger internationally, but it can also lead to deliberate or unintentional manipulation of human beings and not least to the annihilation of the human race itself.

## 2. A plea for an order of mutual peace

In the face of the dangers to peace which are already evident or are only just beginning to emerge, all peoples and states, including those with conflicting orders, ideologies, religions, interests, etc. are called on to enter into partnership to ensure survival. The shared dangers, vulnerabilities, interconnections and dependencies which transcend frontiers make new rules of international life quite indispensable. What is called for is an order of mutual peace, understood as an ongoing process involving the comprehensive realization of democratic structures and ecological ways of life, which recognizes the autonomy and the special interests of the peoples of the South and enables co-operation among all peoples in partnership, with equal rights.

If it were realized, such an order of mutual peace would accept that the only civilized form of security policy is that of the civil interaction and co-operation of partners with equal rights: so it would have no use for armed forces and armaments. But as long as the dangers and risks I have indicated are there, or an order of mutual peace has not been thought out thoroughly enough, far less realized, peoples and states will hardly be prepared to dispense with military precautions altogether. In the light of practice hitherto it can hardly be denied that even the few states which for a great variety of reasons at present have no army do not dispense with military or quasi-military defence altogether. For example, while Costa Rica has abolished its army, it has a strong police force. Constitutionally, Japan is not allowed to maintain armed forces, but it does have so-called defence forces. And even Iceland, which itself has no army, has put itself and its territory at the disposal of NATO as a *quid pro quo*.

What follows from these reflections for the existence, extent and arming of forces in Europe? Suppose that the extent and level of equipment of the forces have hitherto been dictated by external factors, notably the East-West conflict, i.e. that they were adequate for the threat and thus justified and necessary. In that case disarmament is possible, indeed necessary, commensurate with the decline in the threat, the reduction in the conflict, the disbanding of the opposing organizations, i.e. to the degree to which the external factor disappears. But conversely, what follows from the logic of these statements for the new international dangers and risks? A stop to disarmament? Even rearmament? Or a reduction in armaments, albeit limited? And precisely what does this mean for the potential size of armed forces, e.g. in the year 2000?

The extent of the possible dangers of the year 2000 can even less be determined quantitatively than those of the East-West conflict in past years. But if a specific future enemy cannot (or can no longer) be identified, security policy is no longer a quantifiable military policy, but in the future will become an abstract security policy including the use of military means. So the answers to the questions raised can be derived only from the political and conceptual requirements of a future security system which will, or rather should, replace the previous military pacts.

## (a)  Conceptual conclusions for a European security system

At the latest since the accident with the civil nuclear reactor at Chernobyl, it has become clear that at a time when not only economic, political and military linkages, dependencies and/or consequences are constantly increasing, but dangers and crises – whether intentionally or not – have an effect beyond frontiers (economic crises, environmental pollution, radioactive after-effects of a civil reactor accident or a nuclear war), security can no longer be achieved one-sidedly. A nation's own security must always also take into account the security of its neighbours and those standing over against it. In short, security can no longer be had in confrontation; it must be achieved in collaboration. Security is mutual security.

Mutual security is the conceptual and political alternative to deterrence. However, mutual security has fulfilled its conceptual function when the deterrence has been overcome and the disbanding of pacts and blocks has been achieved. To this degree mutual security is a transitional regime. Nevertheless, the insight which leads to mutual security also continues to be valid. Transnational dangers, whether military, economic, ecological or technological, of the kind mentioned in 1*(c)* above, need the insights of trans-national co-operation in partnership, even after the end of the East-West conflict and the disbanding of the pacts. Furthermore, as a transitional concept mutual security aims at the overcoming of threats and dangers to peace 'merely' *in peace*. But must not what needs to be taken into account in normal conditions, e.g. peace, be even more valid in an emergency, i.e. in times of crisis and war? Nuclear radiation does not know national frontiers nor bounds of time.

The rationality which lies in the 'mutual' overcoming of dangers therefore does not end when the emergency occurs. On the contrary, the idea of 'mutual security' must be tested as an approach to the overcoming of conflicts, especially in times of conflict. Thought through consistently to the end, in the long term mutual security thus leads to a system of collective security which also recognizes the military support of its members in emergencies.

The substance of collective security is not completely new. At least the idea of collective security has long appeared in a series of treaties and legal norms. These include articles 52ff. of the United Nations Charter, article 11 of the former Warsaw Pact and also article 24 of the Basic Law of the Federal Republic of Germany.

Looking back over past decades, one certainly cannot deny the relative failure of the idea of collective security in the United Nations. But it would be wrong to say that the idea has finally failed. On the contrary, at the latest since the end of the East-West conflict there has been a need to start from a strengthening of the United Nations and a renaissance of collective security. Examples of this are the unanimity with which in the late summer of 1990 the international community condemned the invasion of Kuwait by Iraq, and the UN Security Council resolved on sanctions backed up with the threat of the use of military force. Nevertheless, it is true that a whole series of disputes even before the Second World War damaged the effectiveness of the then League of Nations, and even after 1945 they prevented the organization of military security in the form of 'collective security', leading to military alliances on the pattern of self-defence or colletive self-defence. These problem issues included and still include not only the effectiveness of military forces but a clear identification of the aggressor, the capacity of the organs of the system of collective security (especially the General Secretary and the Security Council) to decide and act, the institutionalization of compulsory arbitration, and so on.

So what is the way out? In the 1950s there was already discussion of the possibility of regional systems of collective security – which was also permissible under the UN charter – as an intermediary solution leading to a universal system of collective security. However, the proposals for the formation of regional systems were and still are faced with the fundamental problems of achieving collective security. Still, it is easier not only to see these problems – because they are limited to a particular area – but also to deal with them in a political programme. And finally, at the latest since the discussions over mutual security and the structural elimination of aggression, a series of insights and recognitions have developed, acceptable to all sides, which as characteristics of mutual security must also find a way into the formation of collective security.

If it is true that the system of 'collective' security is the logical and consistent development of the basic notion of 'mutual' security, concepts like supremacy and superiority may no longer be understood in the traditional sense, and thus wrongly. 'Superiority' in the system of collective security remains similar to defensive superiority in the regime of mutual superiority. Collective security does not seek collective superiority, but is exclusively aimed at prevention. Internally, in cases of conflict this demands collective sanctions and the renunciation of means of mass destruction of all kinds. Externally, however, prevention is very different from deterrence. It means reducing the perception of threat on the part of possible opponents by well-planned armaments on one's own side which, while superior, are orientated on defence and are structurally incapable of attack.

Similar clarifications and concretizations can also be found in connection with the question of the functioning and mechanisms, or institutionalized guarantees, of a collective system of European security. If the mistakes and weaknesses of the League of Nations and the United Nations are not to be repeated in Europe at a regional level, this means:

— the formulation of contractual and institutional guarantees which contain a strict and automatic obligation to support any victim of aggression;
— the institutionalization of a European Security Council with the undisputed right to restore collective security in the case of aggression;
— the establishment of supra-national forces and the possibility of legal recourse to national troops;

— the building up of institutionalized possibilities for compulsory peaceful elimination of conflicts (anyone who refuses to accept arbitration is an aggressor) and for peaceful change in the direction of an order of mutual peace;

— and not least with a view to a new European peace order in the wider sense: permanent institutions and a variety of consultative mechanisms for multilateral European collaboration in all areas.

### (b) Restructuring as an evolutionary process

The first steps in this direction, especially from the perspective indicated in *(a)* above, can be found in the statement made after the Paris meeting of heads of state on 21 November 1990. In this Paris Charter the following new structures and institutions were resolved on as part of the process:

— a council, consisting of the foreign ministers of the member states;
— a committee of senior officials;
— a secretariat in Prague;
— a centre for preventing conflict in Vienna;
— a bureau for free elections in Warsaw.

However, these resolutions contain more than first cautious steps forward. In the long term they are intended to lead to a European system of collective security. So they must be developed and supplemented with a series of institutions and organs. One could imagine as a model the chief organs of the United Nations and their functions in accordance with articles 52–54 of the UN charter along with articles 7ff. The minimum organs needed would thus be:

— an assembly of members (general assembly)
— a security commission (security council)
— a secretariat (general secretary).

As a further main organ, a European court of justice or the International Court of Justice could assume judicial functions. And on the basis of articles 47ff. of the UN Charter a European general staff committee could be set up to support the security commission.

Suppose one starts by assuming that the military structure of a collective security system will be shaped not only by the renunciation of means of mass destruction but also by:

— the forces being completely or partially supranational;

— the system being orientated both internally and externally on prevention;

— the forces or their weapons being orientated on defence (no offensive potential).

In that case the following steps and measures towards a system of collective European security can not only be imagined but already implemented in an evolutionary process now, i.e. even during the ongoing and provisional existence of NATO.

— the formation of contingents of mixed nationalities and the granting of a free vote on the completion of military service in foreign (allied) forces as well;

— the abandonment of the 'national triad concept' while maintaining the effectiveness of the total system, i.e. developing specialist national forces and dividing the work between them in such a way that aggression by individual states internally or externally become impossible or at least incalculable;

— the rearming of forces with the most modern technologies to provide an effective but defence-orientated potential (structurally with no offensive potential).

If some individual states wanted to seize the chance of being pioneers in the process of creating a new European security system, there is a further possibility on the basis of the measures mentioned above:

— a unilateral, radical reduction of military capacity, armed forces and arms to around a fifth of what they are at present; even a strong European security system (with a 'mere' million soldiers instead of the 4–5 million as hitherto) will hardly require more of an individual state.

These and similar considerations may still sound utopian. But the revolutionary changes in relations between East and West show almost daily that even utopias can become reality.

*Translated by John Bowden*

For a more detailed discussion see Dieter S. Lutz, *Sicherheit 2000*, Baden-Baden 1991.

# Foreigners as an Opportunity

## Jacques Audinet

For centuries, to Europeans a foreigner was another European: the Germans were foreigners to the French, the English to the Latin peoples, the French to the Spanish or the Italians. The word 'foreigner' denoted someone living beyond one's national frontier. These frontiers were crossed only by rare privileged people like statesmen or business-men, artists or dilettantes. The poor who crossed them out of necessity rapidly disguised their origins and melted away into the new host popu-lation. That was, if the frontier did not become the scene of the encounter of masses of men in the murderous confrontations of wars which have punctuated the history of Europe. Beyond Europe there were the colonies and then those unknown lands whose names were contemplated idly on maps. In portraying foreigners history books took up ancient stereotypes, a mixture of admiration and fear, and exalted the originality of each nation. We know now that this was a cramped history, that of a Europe which thought that it was the centre of the world.

Things have changed. History has speeded up and geography embraces the whole planet. Frontiers have become permeable. One only has to go for a walk in any city or town in Europe to see that there are foreigners everywhere. They come from every corner of the world: not only from Europe but from Africa, America or Asia. So much is this the case that the word 'foreigner' has come increasingly to denote the popu-lations of the Third World, arriving with their potential for the labour force, their styles of life and their customs, transforming districts of the major cities into outposts of their distant homeland. They are the new Europeans. And what is the place of these new Europeans in Europe? How can Europe find a place for them? In other words, how do they view Europe and how are they viewed by the Europeans who preceded them in that territory?

## 1. What is the place of foreigners in Europe?

First of all we must note that it is impossible to include in a single
description all those women and men who are now flowing towards
Europe. And Europe itself embraces considerable differences.[1] In 1990
the number of foreign immigrants in Western Europe was estimated at 12
million or about 4% of the total population, unevenly distributed country
by country. This figure includes both migrants within Europe and
emigrants from the Third World. The latter come from North Africa and
continental Africa, southern Asia and the Caribbean, Turkey and the
Middle East. For the first time in the history of Europe they represent a
massive influx of populations who are heterogenous in both origin and
culture. They are concentrated mainly in the industrial regions: Germany,
England, Benelux, France. That is where the questions about the new
Europeans become most acute. This questioning is new and arises where
public opinion becomes convinced that they will never be returning home.
While we must avoid any form of generalization, over and above the
diversity it seems possible to note certain common features in the situation
of those who arrive in Europe.

## 2. Europe: a necessity and a plan

For most of these immigrants Europe is a land of necessity, but at the same
time it is part of a plan. It is a necessity as a political refuge. Europe as a
sanctuary offers security, freedom of opinion and respect for the person, all
of which are unknown in the countries from which these people have had to
flee. Europe offers freedom of expression and respect for human rights,
and thus appears as a welcoming land where, albeit by fits and starts, the
great dream of brotherhood and a reunited humanity is being pursued.
And as the years go by, for a certain number of immigrants the hope of
return becomes blurred and Europe then becomes the new city in which
they plant their tents and build a future.

For economic migrants the situation is different. Forced to cross the seas
to find work, they arrive with their physical strength as their only
resources. The nature of their stay, which is initially temporary and
required solely by the need to send money home, changes from the
moment when a family regrouping enables them to reunite their family.
The rest of the family comes to Europe and puts down roots there. The
idea of going home rapidly disappears. The children will be Europeans.
Nostalgia is replaced by a plan.

And thus begins the long process denoted by the multiple words integration, assimilation, insertion. Each of these words in fact marks the adoption of different positions over the fact of immigration. The word integration seems the most appropriate because it is most open and has most respect for what is at stake. Integration varies depending on the countries and legal systems, but is a social and psychological process. It is the very crucible in which in one way or another the new Europe is being made for these men and women. Described thousands of times in novels and sociological studies, both its direction and the violence bound up with it have become well known. The more immediate problem is coping with an environment which rejects the foreigner in the name of all kinds of prejudice and racism. More personally, there is the problem of the disintegration of one identity, combined with the impossibility for the person concerned fully to take over his or her new identity. This has deep human consequences when parents have to accept that their children will be different and will hand on a different tradition from that received from their ancestors. The host country is inevitably also a testing ground, and this is a test which is undergone in everyday life, behind the façade of legislative organizations and systems.

## From an ethnic bond to a democratic bond

But we cannot stop at these descriptive aspects which I have been able only to touch on. We must try to understand what is at stake for Europe and the new Europeans in what is going on here. What is happening is a transition to modernity. The project of migration is a project of access to modernity. Hence its power and also its violence.[2] To begin with, the majority of new Europeans come from countries which have only recently become nations, from former colonies or empires which have disintegrated and in which the democratic tradition is taking its first tenatative steps, if it exists at all. That is to say that for them the social bond is an ethnic bond and not a political bond, that their vision of the world is religious and not secular, that the identity of the individual, whether man or woman, is fixed in ancestral and unchanging roles. Through the vicissitudes of language, work and education, in two generations they have to cover the course which it took the indigenous European populations two centuries to cover.

To move from an ethnic bond to a national and democratic bond involves a series of painful adjustments, the main of which take place in the family and the environment. In Europe, it is impossible to create protective ghettos for survival, as is still done in certain communities in the United States. There it is possible, at least for a time, for the illusion of the former life to remain. Here the social laws, education, the health systems, call for everyday exchanges in which language becomes the open sesame and in which relations are established by the individual and not through the mediation of the family or clan group. Then living becomes a permanent trade-off between the modes of life inherited from the past and the new possibilities of life as a citizen, both as a producer and a consumer. If the price to pay is a heavy one, the profit is immense; it is that of access to a society of plenty and of security, and a future, especially where children's education is concerned. The bond with the past is then reduced to the hard core of family and religious traditions, while the rest of existence becomes Westernized. This hard core consists of physical practices, rites, cooking, clothing, and will be manifested in a multitude of forms ranging from a falling back on past traditions to the dissolution of these traditions in the new identity. But whatever the form it takes, integration will require a good deal of time and involve much suffering.

Two things need to be noted in such a process, which are specific to Europe: first the political aspect and secondly the secular aspect. Europe is a region in which the nations set store by civil rights. These exist by the will of the citizens, which is the source of their legitimacy and the guarantee of their functioning. This aspect is evident at every level of social organization from school to public, social and cultural activities and universal suffrage. It shapes the citizens of modern democratic states as autonomous individuals, responsible for their decisions and accountable only for themselves before the law. The educational and legislative systems of the various countries of Europe mark out this process in different ways, just as they offer different images of the nation to those who live in their territory. Tomorrow's Europe will be shaped by debates, for example, on whether immigrants should have the right to vote in particular instances or have universal suffrage, and by the image of the Community which is offered. This is not seen in the same way by Germans, French, British or Italians. That raises the question of European citizenship, which is heightened by the presence of immigrants. Daniel Cohn Bendit recently proposed European citizenship for migrant workers.[3] So these would be the avant-garde of what is emerging from the dynamic of the facts, even if it is not yet recognized by the law.

But the other side of such a process is the abandonment of former ethnic and cultural identity. Here it emerges that the ways in which an original community is maintained on European soil is largely illusory. Here again situations differ: for example, British legislation differs from that of France. But it is significant that efforts made to retain a language sometimes prove negative in that they retard or block the process of integration rather than facilitating it. It would seem here that access to modernity cannot be by sectors, and that the project of emigration is a future-orientated one. The failure in various countries of a policy of returning immigrants to their home countries at the end of the 1970s showed the definitive character of this project. More recently, the Gulf War has been revealing in this connection. In this sense the immigrants are the Europeans of the future.

### The traditional universe of secularity

The other specific aspect of Europe is its secularity. Of all the continents of the world, Europe is the one in which the break between society and religion is the oldest and the most established, fixed in legal forms as well as in mentalities. Social relations are regulated by the rationality of common law and no longer by customs and allegiances. The states are lay, and so is everyday life. In other words, religion is no longer the cement of social life, the bond which holds together personal life, collective life and the forces of the cosmos. It is forced back into the sphere of personal decision, and although it is manifested socially, in the end it relates to private life. In other words, living in Europe forces people to apprentice themselves to the European invention of secular life. This involves a redefinition of the religious in society and of personal relations to the religious. Beyond question this is the most decisive and the most painful point. For it necessarily involves conflict and intimately affects personal life.

The solutions which are being worked out here depict a new aspect of the future. They cannot emerge ready-made. And generalizations about the return of the religious or postmodernity are more likely to create confusion than to illuminate the situation. The maintaining of a past, or a nostalgia for the past, which for modernity represents the archaic, cannot be the way forward. In this sense it is impossible to get beyond modernity. Modernity bears within itself its own capacity for renewal and its own capacity for assuming the past by transforming it. And the new Europeans, confronted head-on with its liberating force, show us all the sphere of our responsibilities.

## 3. The foreigner reveals Europe

How does Europe understand these immigrants? What models does Europe have for reflecting on such a new fact and recognizing its fruitfulness? For from now on it is impossible to ignore the magnitude of the phenomenon and its inevitability.

### Archaic categories

As always when people are faced with novelty, archaic categories resurface. These categories centre on two themes, those of the barbarian invasion and of reverse colonization. According to some people, history is repeating itself, and Europe is in process of re-experiencing what happened to Rome with the infiltration of the barbarians and then their arrival *en masse*, a process which will lead to the same destiny, that of the end of the empire. Or history has reversed itself, and those to whom Europe brought civilization are turning on the hand which fed them. These themes are not just those of a low-grade nationalist propaganda. They also nourish a strategic reflexion and dominate choices.[4] Reopening scars which have not properly healed, they could feed a variety of forms of racism with violence and the incomprehension which that brings in train. Racism is a protean monster, and it is not enough to call oneself anti-racist to get rid of it.[5]

The permanence of these themes and the way in which they recur invites Europe to ask itself questions about itself, i.e. about its relations with others.[6] For if such perspectives are destructive for others, they are equally destructive for Europeans. In fact they invite Europeans to deny the very originality of Europe, namely the long toil by which modern Europe has been constructed and which, thanks to law and rationality, has brought it clear of violent relations between its peoples. It is not that this work is finished, or that Europe is free of violence. But at the cost of the wars which it has unleashed, Europe has had to learn that human relations can take another form, namely respect for treaties and human rights. To want to return from this to race-relations, to exalt the primacy of race once again, and to conceive of culture[7] as the prerogative of a single white tribe would be to go backwards and to lose what makes up the originality of Europe. In this sense the new arrivals on European soil are the best evidence of Europe's fidelity to itself.

## Pursuing the invention of Europe[8]

This is what the Europeans are invited to do by the new arrivals. In fact it proves that Europe has always been formed by the contribution of foreigners. The phenomenon which is unfolding today strikes us by virtue of its magnitude and its rapidity, but Europe has always been a host land. Its history is specifically that of a mixture of populations. The new factor is that today's arrivals no longer come from neighbouring countries but from distant groups and cultures which radicalize the foreign character of the other and alter balances which hitherto had seemed unalterable. Thus France, the well-beloved daughter of the church, is a country in which the second religion is Islam. So Europe is forced to accept the truth of its identity, that of a continent made up of multiple populations which in the course of time have come to pool their riches and construct the countries that we know.

Hence reflection on the novelty of Europe invites us to go beyond words each of which has its riches and limits. That is the case with the word intercultural. While it suggests diversity and the overcoming of a sense of the foreign, it remains an empty form unless it is given specific content. It risks offering the lure of illusory ease if it masks the resistance of reality. And Europe is particularly resistant to the acceptance of foreign cultures. The European nations have been formed on the basis of exclusive categories. Exclusion of the foreigner draws on archaic categories which, though masked, are always active. Exclusion of the infidel in the name of the faith presupposes communal exclusion of the impure in the name of the homogeneity of an illusory purity. The expulsion of the Moors and the Jews from Spain in 1492 was justified by purity of blood, thus identifying territory, race and nation at the dawn of modern Europe. Finally, there is the fascination with a unity and a universality which was the justification for the colonial enterprise. Such categories may have disappeared from explicit discourse but surveys of attitudes bring out their latent presence. They sometimes remain as a kind of foundation which is hard to identify explicitly but which is nevertheless there, an attitude to which people hold because it seems to constitute the identity of Europe, to be what made Europe great in the past, but also to be the basis for solidarity, not to mention generosity. So it becomes difficult to put these categories in question.

However, there are categories which can be used both for the immigrants and for the construction of the New Europe. At the very moment when Europe is seeing foreign populations flowing on to its territory and questioning each nation from within, these nations themselves are seeing their traditional identity overturned from outside by the very logic of the European project. This goes beyond economics and politics. In fact it affects both the image which Europe gives itself and its view of its place in the world. Now at last categories of universality, unity or identity have to be taken up again within the design of the world which is beginning to emerge – in reality and not just in the fantasies of new world orders. The presence of foreigners in the countries of Europe then shows the face of a world which from now on can only be one. That is what the clear-headed authorities in the Third World countries never cease to recall.

### There are virtually no models

Europe does not recognize itself in the model of the American melting-pot. Here space and time are both different. It is impossible to live with only a future orientation when every inch of territory bears the mark of history. And the frontier is not out in the West, but in the heart of Europe, constantly transgressed and reconstructed.[9] But America, this time South America, does offer another model. It is that of cross-breeding, i.e. of the 'mixture' which has been produced throughout Latin America since the sixteenth century. This is a mixture denoted by words with different nuances in each of the European languages, sometimes with connotations of rejection. However, it is a mixture which was the fruit of the European enterprise and which through the violence of destruction allowed the birth of a new society.[10] Today the word has been restored to favour in the term 'cultural cross-breeding'.

Cultural cross-breeding does not stress the ethnic dimension, which was the factor in the sixteenth-century, but the interhuman dimension. It makes it possible to take a positive view of what is in process of happening. It involves the encounter of two different entities which gives birth to a third entity that inherits from them while at the same time being new. Cultural cross-breeding is perhaps an alternative to negative racist attitudes. In short, Europe can be thought of as a breeding ground, accepting a new breed by accepting that it is made up of a mixture of all the riches of humanity, coming together on its soil. Cross-breeding emphasizes two conditions for a constructive relationship between peoples: the time that is needed and the suffering that is inevitable. The category of cross-breeding does not have the aseptic character which 'intercultural' risks having. Cross-breeding happens physically and often through violence. That is why mixed couples are perhaps the symbolic and paradigmatic context of what is happening in Europe. We know that for every couple and perhaps even more for mixed couples there is an inner frontier which sometimes cannot be crossed but which is nevertheless lifegiving.

At a time when Europe is preparing to commemorate the quincentenary of the year 1492, which was at the same time, for better or worse, the symbolic year of the expansion of Europe and that of the beginning of the modern world, for the first time Europe is aware of being confronted with unexpected phenomena on a world scale. Europeans have the responsibility for constructing a modern Europe, not one of archaisms; a Europe of openness rather than particularisms, of human rights rather than slavery. Europeans are not alone in having to do that. Whether they like it or not, the destiny of the whole of the world is involved in the adventure, and the foreigners are in Europe.

*Translated by John Bowden*

## Notes

1. Cf. *Six manières d'être européens*, ed. Dominique Schnapper and Henri Mendras, Paris 1990.

2. Here I am drawing on the remarkable work by Dominique Schnapper, *La France de l'Intégration. Sociologie de la nation en 1990*, Paris 1991; its documentation and scope go far beyond the situation in France.

3. 'Un Entretien avec M. Daniel Cohn-Bendit', *Le Monde*, 27 June 1991.

4. Cf. e.g. Jean-Christophe Rufin, *L'empire et les nouveau barbares*, Paris 1991.

5. Cf. Pierre-Andre Taguieff (ed.), *Face au racisme* (2 vols.), Paris 1991.

6. Cf. the fine book by Tsvetan Todorov, *Nous et les autres*, Paris 1990.

7. We might note the double meaning of the word culture and the riches or the ambiguity of this word, depending on the sense given it. Cf. Norbert Elias, *La civilization des moeurs*, Paris 1973.

8. Thus the title of the book by Olivier Todd, *L'Invention de l'Europe*, Paris 1990.

9. A colloquy held at the University of Metz in October 1990 by the Centre de Recherche Pensée Chrétienne was entitled 'The Future at the Frontier. The Spiritual Destiny of Europe'. The proceedings are to be published.

10. Cf. Virgil Elizondo, *The Future is Mestizo. Life Where Cultures Meet*, Oak Park, Illinois 1988.

# What About the Garden? The Ecological Dimensions of the European Home

## Lukas Vischer

### 1.

Talk of the 'European home' has recently lost much of its attraction. For a while great hopes were attached to it, but meanwhile it has become clear to even the most incorrigible optimists that the way to comprehensive unity will be long and laborious – if it ever reaches its goal at all. A few years ago, when there was movement on the entrenched fronts and the constellation which had dominated Europe since the Second World War was being put in question, it seemed to many people that the vision of a European home could become a tangible reality in the near future. In the meantime, however, it has become much clearer just how complex the situation was. Those who had not long known it at least know it now: to build a home, it is not enough to break down walls; rather, what is needed is a common architectural will. But here agreement has clearly yet to be achieved.

Moreover, so far the factor which most threatens the future of Europe has not yet fully been taken into account in the considerations and plans of the authorities. The *ecological crisis* is still at best treated as a secondary issue. Certainly we may regard as progress the fact that meanwhile its existence has been recognized in all parts of Europe. Until relatively recently, the official view in Eastern Europe was that ecological concern was a psychosis of Western society. But the insight has yet to progress far enough to become the priority. The debate over the 'European home' is still predominantly carried on in economic, political and military categories. Certainly, everyone talks about the ecological crisis, but it is still always regarded as an 'additional problem'; perhaps it is the decisive question in the long term, but precisely because it is a long-term problem, the more immediate problems may with good reason claim priority. However, in fact this is to get things the wrong way round: while the discussions over the future of Europe, which are apparently so important, are being struggled through, in the background another clock is ticking away. The survival of humankind on this planet is in question. In view of this fact, the remark that one keeps hearing, 'at the moment we have more urgent business', seems almost eerie. It is utterly wrong to think that there are more important concerns – and that a new commitment to the preservation of creation may be left until the step after next. The ecological crisis must now, already, be an integral part of a responsible policy on Europe. Indeed the quality of any European policy will need to be measured by the consistency with which it incorporates the ecological dimension. If a home is to be livable in, a change of course is needed. A home by itself does not guarantee life.

There is no need to describe the threats here yet again. The list has been set out often enough: plundering of resources, pollution of the earth, forests, air and water – in hundreds of ways the nature which supports us is having its supportive power reduced. Here the real danger lies in the accumulation of incursions into nature and attacks on it. The individual problems may find a solution, and there are scenarios for the solving every single problem. But the real difficulty is to see where the spiritual and moral power will come from to tackle the many different ecological problems all at the same time and bring a solution nearer. As yet there is no scenario for the construction of an ecologically responsible world, and even if there were, we would still have to reckon with the possibility that it would be deeply disrupted and upset by unforeseen historical events. The Gulf War is a good example of such an incident.

In this connection special mention must be made of the warming of the atmosphere by the greenhouse effect and the climatic changes which could result from this. The ecological crisis is focussed most clearly in this process. Whereas human intervention elsewhere has an effect only on particular spheres of human life, here we have a global process: the conditions of life all over the earth are being changed by human beings.

## 2.

But what about Europe today? Readiness to face the crisis is still very limited. Given the magnitude of the problem, the measures which are being taken are hardly more than cosmetic.

The damage done by the crisis is more visible in the Eastern part of Europe than in the West. The almost systematic neglect of the problem, extending over years, has meant that in many places the disaster is manifest. At this point, too, the centralistic system of state socialism has shown its inability to tackle new developments constructively. The challenge posed by the ecological crisis has notoriously been overlooked. This was one of the main focal points for opposition to the system. Poets, intellectuals and grass-roots groups made the preservation of the environment their theme and with increasing openness criticized the devastating consequences of a planned economy working in a short-sighted way. The protests against the destruction of Lake Baikal, against the Nagyvaros dam and the building of the Trans-Caucasus railway in Georgia, will go down in the history of the ecological movement as symbols of resistance. As a result, the changes in Eastern Europe have also taken on an ecological dimension. Today there is agreement that large-scale ecological clearing-up is one of the most urgent tasks of the new governments. However, the question is how far the political forces which have established themselves in the revolution really recognize the task either. The movements which first offered resistance are today again in the same political wilderness as in former years.

What about the West? There is a great temptation to misuse the ecological mess in the Eastern European states which is becoming increasingly obvious as a justification for Western attitudes. For no matter what may be said about the ecological dangers and damage in the West, an even worse picture can be painted in the East. And in fact there can be hardly any doubt that the basis for an ecologically responsible attitude in the West was far more favourable. The democratic rights which exist in Western society made an early debate on the problems possible. It was possible for awareness of the ecological crisis to grow, and some first measures could be enforced on the basis of the increasing public consensus. The significance of the fact that those who cause ecological damage are to some degree accountable to public opinion cannot be rated too highly.

However, it would be premature to proclaim the superiority of the West too quickly. For that can only be claimed when the Western states have shown that they also have long-term solutions to offer for overcoming the crisis, and so far there is no sign of this. In the long term the problems have not been solved in the West any more than they have in the East. Far from it being possible to speak of a clearly developed awareness of the ecological problems, the measures which are being proposed keep coming to grief on short-term considerations and interests.

Some examples may make this clear:

— There is almost no dispute over the need to use less energy, above all energy from fossil fuels, yet governments continue to reckon on an annual increase in energy consumption.

— The insight has indeed been established that there are limits to mobility and that above all private transport must not be extended further, yet the European Community reckons on a 30% increase in the volume of traffic by the year 2005. It is said that air travel will even double.

— It is indeed generally acknowledged that the mountain of waste must not grow any higher and that above all toxic waste must be reduced to a minimum, yet waste continues to be produced which will cause trouble not only for us but also for future generations.

### 3.

The ecological crisis has global dimensions. The European home is part of all humankind and therefore also shares responsibility for the future and the survival of the whole human race, especially the countries of the South. The ecological crisis has led to a tremendous intensification of the North-South conflict. It is of crucial importance for Europe to become aware of its role in this worldwide context.

First of all it must be remembered that not all parts of humankind have contributed to the ecological catastrophe to the same extent. The share of the North is far greater than that of the South. The modern aggressive, exploitative and destructive treatment of creation has its social and spiritual roots in the civilizations of the North, and even today the plundering of the planet is caused above all by the industrialized nations of Europe and North America.

So it is at least misleading when people occasionally say that 'human' intervention is endangering the foundations of life on earth. This way of putting it disguises the fact that the subject of ecological destruction is not 'human beings' generally but a particular part of the human race. It is primarily the representatives of modern scientific and technological society who have brought this disaster upon the world. Europe bears a world-wide responsibility, as a result of both its history and its present life-style.

The conflict is further intensified by the fact that in many respects the ecological crisis affects the countries of the South more severely. Having already been excluded from the economic advantages that Western civilization could have brought, they must now bear the main burden of ecological destruction. Whereas the West is in principle in a position to meet the danger, they are largely exposed to it. Whereas the West can develop new technologies which respect the environment, they have neither the scientific nor the technological and financial means to achieve a new orientation. No matter how aware people are becoming of the ecological crisis, any initiative is being paralysed, if not destroyed, by poverty.

The best example of this new aspect of the North-South conflict is the problem of global warming. Responsibility for the greenhouse gases which result in the rise in average temperature is unequally divided. Thus about 75% of the $CO_2$ emissions come from the industrialized nations with their relatively small population, and only about 25% from the poor countries of the South. If the $CO_2$ emissions of the last century are totalled up, the difference becomes even greater. However, the countries of the South will be the first victims of the climatic changes which will in all probability come about and perhaps have already begun: the general unpredictability of the weather, the spread of the deserts and the increase in storms and floods. The Second World Conference on the Climate in November 1990 left no doubt about this: the consequences of global warming especially affect those who in any case already suffer economic disadvantages.

This example shows very clearly the responsibility of the industrialized nations. The almost inevitable conclusion to be drawn from it is that the emissions of $CO_2$, or specifically the energy consumption of the North, are not just ecologically irresponsible but at the same time represent a new form of exploitation. By continuing to pursue the plan to achieve a technological society, the industrial nations are doing irreparable damage to the nations of the South.

When the West gradually became aware of the ecological crisis, at first the countries of the South were sceptical. Was there a real danger, or were the industrialized nations simply looking for a pretext to avoid responsibility for the poor nations? Was the spectre of the ecological crisis perhaps even being used as an argument for withholding economic development from them? The clearer the damage became, the more the mood changed. It was increasingly recognized that economic development is meaningless in the long term without simultaneous measures to protect the environment. That makes the question how far the industrialized nations are really prepared to perceive this new responsibility all the more urgent.

They are still a long way from such a perception. Even in circles which are ecologically open, the global dimension of eco-justice still plays a subordinate role. And yet the discussion over the ecological crisis must inevitably lead to the insight that only a new commitment to the poor countries can ensure the survival of humanity. Just as justice and peace belong together, so too justice and the safeguarding of creation cannot be separated. To the degree that the economic exploitation of the poor nations is continued, the foundation of life not only in the South but ultimately also in the North will be endangered. The ecological crisis is therefore not only leading to an intensification of the North-South conflict but at the same time making a comprehensive solution all the more urgent. It has rightly been said that the ecological crisis has made both the North and the South equally vulnerable. In the face of the catastrophe which threatens, the North is not just in the position of the unshakably stronger party.

However, virtually nothing of this could be detected at the Second World Conference on the Climate. On the scientific side the requirements were clear: to avoid the danger of far-reaching climatic changes, from now on the annual global consumption of energy must be reduced by between 1% and 2%; because the industrial nations are the main users, their contribution to this reduction must be proportionately higher. The delegations from the industrialized nations, above all the United States and the Soviet Union (supported by Saudi Arabia), remained adamant. They declared that they were not prepared either to limit their own consumption or to finance any compensation or relief for the countries of the South. The Western European nations agreed to stabilize their energy consumption at the 1990 level by the year 2000. The development of a world convention on the climate was unanimously approved. The text was to be available by the middle of 1991 and to be circulated among the states for ratification. However, given the resistance among the rich countries it remains doubtful whether an effective text will be produced, and if it is, whether the states will approve it and observe it.

The countries of the Third World pose a special challenge to Europe. Will the European countries fight their way through to the insight that the way forward can be found only within the framework of a comprehensive community of all nations? Or will they succumb to the temptation to limit their attention to their own garden and perhaps even protect it against outsiders with a high wall?

## 4.

What role have the churches played in this area? Much has been set in motion in recent years. The question of the understanding of creation has again become a theme in theological circles. Numerous members of the churches are active in the ecological movement – as individuals or as groups – out of Christian conviction. So there is no doubt that in the face of the ecological crisis in the churches, at many points new approaches must be made on both a theological and a practical level.

However, at an official level the attitude of the churches is still characterized by great restraint. Certainly there is hardly a church which has not spoken out on the theme in one way or another by now. But the great majority of churches hardly get beyond words. The fear of being drawn into political controversies has a restraining, if not a paralysing effect. Again and again it is pointed out that the church has an all-embracing mission and that it must not move on the level of a Green party or an environmental organization.

Furthermore, sensitivity to the ecological crisis varies both from confession to confession and from culture to culture. Whereas for example the Protestant Churches of Germany have for many years had officers with special responsibility for environmental questions, in other churches the theme is still hardly discussed. And whereas questions like the reduction of mobility can certainly be discussed openly in countries like the Netherlands or Germany, in other countries like France they are dismissed with a shrug of the shoulders. This makes it difficult for the churches to collaborate and bear a joint witness on a European level.

The 1989 European ecumenical assembly 'Peace in Justice' in Basel brought out this situation clearly. Great emphasis was put on the theme, and its urgency was also underlined by the presence of numerous church groups. In clarity, both the message and the report of the Assembly leave nothing to be desired. And yet even after Basel a new movement has not yet emerged among the churches. Even now they are hardly more than a mirror of society: just as in society the ecological movement is supported by particular parties and organizations, so here too it remains limited to spontaneous initiatives.

### 5.

What kind of a contribution can the churches make? The following considerations may indicate the direction:

(a) The first and perhaps the most important contribution is constantly to remind people of the magnitude of the crisis. However much the theme is discussed in public, at the decisive moment there is a great temptation to suppress the challenge or to evade the issue by arguments which play it down. The churches must have the inner freedom, the courage and above all the stubbornness to resist this and to keep spelling out the implications of the crisis. They cannot engage in this task without sooner or later coming up against a difficulty. How can they raise a warning voice without disappointing the expectations which are placed in them? For are they not expected to be a treasury of hope in this time of uncertainty and anxiety? The churches are easily misled by this pressure and as a result blur the challenge by religious statements about hope. But the freedom which the gospel brings must be shown precisely in the way in which Christians can face reality.

(b) Beyond question the implications also include the insight that the ecological crisis calls for a reorientation not only of society but also of each of its members. The Ecumenical Assembly in Basel rightly spoke of the need for a 'conversion'. All previous conception about life have been put in question. It is important to stress this insight because there is still a widespread view that the crisis can only be overcome by the further development of science and technology. But the tasks of the churches include the need to unmask this expectation as superstition. Unavoidable as the contribution of science and technology is, it is an illusion to start from the assumption that the present course can be continued unchanged. A radical reorientation in dealing with creation is called for.

(c) The obligation to preserve the gifts of creation follows not only from responsibility for people living today but also from respect for future generations. God's covenant applies not only to Noah and those with him but also to his 'descendants and all living creatures upon earth' (Gen. 9.9). Not only the present generation, but also the generations which will come after us, have 'rights' which must be perceived and taken up now. The gifts of creation are also intended for them. One of the tasks of the churches is to think through this responsibility down to its last consequence and remind both themselves and the public of it. It is striking, for example, that even scientific calculations and scenarios hardly go beyond the time of our grandchildren, as though present-day conduct which puts in question the survival of following generations were ethically irrelevant.

(d) When future generations are mentioned, we spontaneously think of our own descendants. But God's covenant applies to the whole human race: 'When the bow is seen in the clouds, I will remember my covenant which is between me and every living creature which is upon the earth' (Gen. 9.13f). This insight is particularly topical, because the ecological crisis bears within itself the seed of radical carelessness. As long as we survive, what does the future of other peoples matter to us?

Considerations of this kind are emerging above all in the industrialized countries of the North and are increasingly spoken out aloud. It is said more and more often that some countries have only very limited chances of survival; is it not more sensible to concentrate on those that can help themselves? The churches have to oppose such considerations resolutely right from the beginning. A European home which rests on such considerations cannot stand; it would lose its soul.

*(e)* Beyond doubt another of the tasks of the churches is to reflect on their own tradition. How are we to interpret the fact that the civilization in which the ecological crisis has its origin was shaped by Christianity in particular? Does the reason for the crisis really lie in the biblical message itself? Or has this message been misunderstood and misused in the course of history? What, for example, about the role of human beings towards their fellow creatures? Precisely on the basis of the biblical message, must there not be much more resolute talk not only of human rights but also of the rights of nature?

*(f)* The new orientation which is called for by the ecological crisis inevitably also raises the question of life-style. What is the responsible way of dealing with the gifts of creation? It is increasingly being realized that our claims on natural resources must be drastically reduced. More and more voices, also and particularly from the secular side, speak of the need for an ascetic life-style, which for many people is a terrifying and oppressive perspective. The contribution the churches can make here is obvious. For does not the gospel teach that a simpler life which is not dependent on external goods leads to more freedom and greater human availability? In the face of the ecological crisis, the ascetic tradition of the churches takes on new topicality.

*(g)* Finally, the decisive question is whether these insights can be translated into a movement which goes beyond confessional limits and is able to bear a common witness in the European sphere. Insights into the ecological crisis must be not only formulated but also lived out and witnessed. A common perception of this responsibility might perhaps become the starting point for a new phase of the ecumenical movement.

*Translated by John Bowden*

# How Religious is Europe?

## Jan Kerkhofs

There have been far-reaching changes in European society since World War II. Automation, new systems of communication, mass tourism, the thoroughgoing socialization of education and culture, the steady improvement in health care, an economic expansion which has only briefly been interrupted, have made Western Europe one of the richest areas in the world. This acceleration of history – one cannot call it anything else – has deeply influenced the European picture of humanity. Freedom and equality are increasing, and so too, therefore, is individualism. Relations between the sexes are becoming increasingly open as a result of the progress in women's emancipation. Class conflict is lessening as a result of better training generally and a levelling off of differences in income. The European Community was and remains the motive force for this whole process throughout Western Europe and it has a strong attraction for Eastern Europe, which is in process of liberating itself.

This whole development has had a marked effect on the views and conduct of the average European, above all in the ethical and religious spheres. 'Secularization', understood as emancipation from religious and church traditions and structures, is no longer limited to the stratum of those with higher education or economic power. It has penetrated everywhere.

In this article I want to restrict myself to a summary account of the information about religion offered by the surveys of values and norms which have been made by the European Value Systems Study Group Foundation. With the help of university and specialist institutions, in 1981 the EVSSG[1] organized a comprehensive survey of Western Europe which was partially repeated in 1990/1991 and is now also being extended to some Eastern European countries.

In 1990 questions were asked about the relative importance of a number of areas of values. The table below, which lists the proportions of those who gave the answers 'very important' or 'important', will serve as a background to the further more detailed discussion which follows.[2]

Table 1
Importance of areas of values (in percentages)

|  | Europe* | Belgium | Spain | Poland | Sweden |
|---|---|---|---|---|---|
| Family | 96 | 95 | 98 | 99 | 97 |
| Friends | 90 | 90 | 91 | 79 | 97 |
| Work | 87 | 89 | 92 | 95 | 96 |
| Leisure time | 82 | 85 | 82 | 82 | 95 |
| Religion | 49 | 45 | 53 | 87 | 27 |
| Politics | 34 | 25 | 20 | 34 | 45 |

We may note in passing that in Western Europe neither income nor profession nor place of abode (town or country) explains the differences in values, nor even gender, except to a very limited degree in the case of religion. Only age is a variable which can explain a significant number of differences.

## 1. The 'Christians'

More than three out of every four Western Europeans claim to belong to a religious confession (76.9%); 75.2% say that they had a religious upbringing at home. Of those who belong to a religious confession, 72.6% are Catholic, 22.8% Protestant and 4.2% belong to another religion. Of those who say that they do not belong to a confession, 36.9% say that they are Catholic, 16.5% Protestant, 5% members of another religion, and 32.5% have never belonged to a confession (9.2% did not reply).

In Poland 97% call themselves Catholic. In what used to be East Germany, around 25% say that they are Christians (4% Catholic). Depending on the sources, in Hungary 71% (or 61%) say that they are Catholics and 26% (or 20%) Protestants. In Rumania the number of Catholics is estimated at 14% and of Protestants at 5%. According to the EVSSG investigation, in Bulgaria 34% claim to belong to a confession; of these, 75% are Orthodox, 20% Muslim, 4% Protestant and 0.3% Catholic. For Yugoslavia the figures are 35% Orthodox, 25% Catholic and 10% Muslim.[3]

However, from a social and cultural perspective 'being Christian' is a very ambiguous term. By no means all 'Christians' believe in God and few find God very important. The following table illustrates this:

Table 2
Belief in God (in percentages) and the importance of God – on a ten-point
scale

|                   | Europe* | Belgium | Spain | Poland | Sweden |
|-------------------|---------|---------|-------|--------|--------|
| Belief in God     | 70.5    | 63.0    | 80.7  | 94.6   | 45.2   |
| Importance of God | 5.68    | 5.22    | 6.25  | 8.32   | 3.75   |

The difference from the USA is significant: in 1981 94% there believed in
God and the importance of God was given more than 8.00 on the ten-point
scale.

## 2. 'Religious' people

Not all 'Christians' say that they are 'religious' and not all those who regard
themselves as 'religious' claim to be Christians. The number of 'Christians'
is greater than the number of 'religious people'. This somewhat subtle
picture is given by the answers to a question which allows three options: 'I
am a religious person,' 'I am not a religious person,' 'I am a convinced
atheist.'

Less than two out of three persons claim to be religious. Compared with
1981 their number is decreasing, although to a lesser degree in southern
Europe. Only in Belgium is there a slight increase in the number of
committed atheists (from 4% to 7%), while only France with 10–11%
clearly exceeds the European average of 5% (in 1981 and 1990). Even
among the younger age-groups few call themselves 'convinced atheists'.
After years of Communism there are only 1% of 'convinced atheists' in
Poland, and Bulgaria seems to have no more of them than Belgium and
Sweden.

Table 3
Religious attitude (in percentages)

|                      | Europe* | Belgium | Spain | Poland | Sweden |
|----------------------|---------|---------|-------|--------|--------|
| Religious person     | 61      | 61      | 63    | 90     | 31     |
| Not a religious person | 28    | 22      | 28    | 2.5    | 62     |
| Convinced atheist    | 5       | 7       | 4     | 1      | 7      |
| Don't know           | 7       | 10      | 4     | 6      |        |

As in France, Great Britain and West Germany, in Scandinavia only a few
people call themselves religious. But – and here we find a very complicated
question – to what extent does a word like 'religion' have the same meaning

in the different countries? Scientific discussion of the international comparability of surveys has scarcely begun.

A number of studies, for example in Germany, Benelux and France, point to new forms of religion, above all among the young. Whereas 'religious' has a predominantly Christian and even Catholic connotation in Ireland and Italy, elsewhere another meaning is developing. 'New age' movements and a kind of 'ecological religion', sometimes taking up process theology, are replacing the traditional Christian understanding of religion. A number of new forms seem to have a strong eschatological streak. One cannot avoid the impression that the traditionally strong emphasis on 'transcendence' is shifting more in the direction of immanence, the experience of nature, cosmic religion, and personal psychological experiences.

For the first time in a large-scale investigation, in 1981 and in 1990 a question was asked about belief in reincarnation. An analysis of the factors shows that this belief is detached from other beliefs. Further study is needed here. However, it does appear that in 1981 more Catholics and Protestants who went to church every week believed in reincarnation (30–35%) than the average population (around 20% in 1981 and 1990). In Sweden there is hardly any difference between the percentages of those who believe in resurrection (21%) and those who believe in reincarnation (20%). In Poland, where 64% say that they believe in resurrection, 32% believe in reincarnation.

It is usually assumed that religious people pray, meditate or do something similar. From the 1990 survey it seems that in many countries people pray never or hardly ever, even when they call themselves religious.

### Table 4
### Frequency of prayer (in percentages)

1. Do you ever spend any time in prayer, meditation, reflection or the like?

|  | Europe* | Belgium | Spain | Poland | Sweden |
|---|---|---|---|---|---|
| Yes | 59.5 | 53.0 | 60.5 | 85.5 | 33.6 |
| No | 36.6 | 43.1 | 36.3 | 9.4 | 66.4 |

2. Apart from religious services, how often do you pray to God?

|  | Europe* | Belgium | Spain | Poland | Sweden |
|---|---|---|---|---|---|
| Often | 23.4 | 16.1 | 27.7 | 53.1 | 9.6 |
| Sometimes | 24.7 | 22.7 | 27.9 | 25.9 | 15.0 |
| Almost never, only in need | 21 | 18.6 | 20.5 | 15.2 | 24.4 |
| Never | 28.3 | 38.1 | 22.8 | 3.8 | 49.1 |

Longitudinal investigations, e.g. in Germany and Belgium, suggest that family prayer is steadily decreasing. There too religion is becoming increasingly individualized.


### 3. Christian believers

'Christianity' and 'Christendom' do not coincide. Of course it is impossible to measure personal 'belief' in sociological terms. But answers to the survey show clear trends in views about traditional belief. Among those who regard themselves as believing Christians there is a great difference over assent to traditionally accepted points of belief. There are also regional differences of emphasis, which reflect the distinctive history of the local churches. All these differences also colour the sometimes sharp polarization within the churches.[4]

Questions were asked about the traditional content of faith and about faith in a personal God.

### Table 5
#### Assent to belief in (in percentages)

|                 | Europe* | Belgium | Spain | Poland | Sweden |
|-----------------|---------|---------|-------|--------|--------|
| The soul        | 61      | 52      | 60    | 72     | 58     |
| Sin             | 57      | 41      | 57    | 83     | 31     |
| Life after death| 43      | 37      | 42    | 62     | 38     |
| Heaven          | 41      | 30      | 48    | 66     | 31     |
| Resurrection    | 33      | 27      | 33    | 64     | 21     |
| The devil       | 25      | 17      | 28    | 29     | 12     |
| Hell            | 23      | 15      | 27    | 35     | 8      |

Between 1981 and 1990 traditional belief has declined in Western Europe. Attempts to investigate to what extent 'alternative' forms of belief are coming into being have yet to produce a result. However, the prevailing individualism seems to exclude more comprehensive new 'systems'. Everyone cooks their own religious brew.

Of course 'God' can mean many things. For Christian believers God is a personal reality, the 'God of Abraham, Isaac and Jacob', as Blaise Pascal confessed, but quite different from any human concept of person. The 'Our Father' illuminates the 'personal' relationship of the followers of Jesus to God. According to the survey, only 38% of people in Western Europe see God as a person (as opposed to 83% in the USA in 1981). The table below illustrates the difference between views within Europe:

Table 6
Views about God (in percentages)

|  | Europe* | Belgium | Spain | Poland | Sweden |
|---|---|---|---|---|---|
| There is a personal God | 38 | 29 | 50 | 78 | 15 |
| There is a kind of life-force or spirit | 33 | 20 | 27 | 5 | 44 |
| Don't know what to think | 15 | 29 | 13 | 13 | 17 |
| Don't think there is a God or life-giving force | 10 | 14 | 7 | 2 | 69 |
| No answer | 4 | 8 | 3 | 2 | 4 |

In fact this table gives a good picture of the more or less advanced secularization of Europe, with striking regional differences. For theologians it is evident here how difficult it is to preach the God of the Bible who is at the same time the Father, concerned for every man and woman, and the immanent source of the creation in which 'we live, move and have our being' (Paul in Acts 17.28).

## 4. Church allegiance

In Europe, religious attitudes are still strongly expressed in church allegiance. Great regional differences can be seen here, and the general trend points to a progressive decline, above all among the youngest age groups. This is more marked among women, although they are still more involved with the church, than among men.

Church allegiance (or the absence of it) is expressed in attitudes and views. In Europe* rather less than half say they have 'much confidence' or 'confidence' in the churches (less than in politics, the European Community, the educational system, the army and social security). In Poland the score on confidence rises to 83%. There are great differences between Poland, Ireland, Italy and Switzerland on the one hand and Great Britain, Scandinavia, West Germany and the Netherlands on the other (between 4% and 30%).

Different answers were given to the question whether it was thought that a person's own church in their own country gave meaningful answers to certain problems:

Table 7
Church's answers to questions (in percentages)

| | Europe* | Belgium | Spain | Poland | Sweden |
|---|---|---|---|---|---|
| Moral problems and personal needs | 36 | 30 | 39 | 67 | 19 |
| Family issues | 32 | 27 | 38 | 71 | 14 |
| Spiritual needs | 54 | 42 | 50 | 80 | 51 |
| Controversial social problems | 27 | 20 | 28 | 38 | 12 |

This does not mean that in some spheres people no longer expect the churches to become involved in public debate, but this is clearly expected less in issues relating to personal life. Only a minority expects the churches to be involved in the sphere of personal conscience.

Table 8
Do you think it right that the churches should speak out on (in percentages), in Europe*

| | Yes | No |
|---|---|---|
| Third world problems | 76 | 18 |
| Racial discrimination | 67 | 26 |
| Euthanasia | 56 | 35 |
| Disarmament | 54 | 38 |
| Ecology | 51 | 41 |
| Abortion | 50 | 43 |
| Unemployment | 45 | 48 |
| Sex outside marriage | 39 | 53 |
| Homosexuality | 34 | 57 |
| Government policy | 22 | 70 |

In the meantime many of the churches continue to be regarded as religious service centres for marking important moments of life. On the question whether people personally think it important that these moments should be marked with formal religious observances Europe presents the following picture:

| | Yes | No | Don't know |
|---|---|---|---|
| Baptism | 69 | 26 | 5 |
| Marriage | 72 | 23 | 4 |
| Funeral | 77 | 18 | 4 |

There are the great, classic differences between countries: higher figures in Ireland, Poland and Italy, lower figures in the Netherlands, France, West Germany, Great Britain, Scandinavia and Belgium. The great majority of people want a church funeral, but in various countries the majority of young people do not want their children to be baptized.

In the sociology of religion, Sunday churchgoing, even if not regular, has traditionally been used as a barometer of church allegiance. However, as a criterion it is now being viewed with much more caution. In assessing the table below one must take into account that the actual figures are usually several percentage points lower than those arising from the interviews:

Table 9
Sunday churchgoing (in percentages)

|  | Europe* | Belgium | Spain | Poland | Sweden |
|---|---|---|---|---|---|
| At least once a week | 23 | 23 | 33 | 66 | 4 |
| Once a month | 11 | 8 | 8 | 18 | 6 |
| Less than once a year | 10 | 8 | 25 | 4 | 17 |
| Never, almost never | 32 | 44 | 22 | 3 | 49 |

Women still go to church more often than men, and those with right-wing politics more often than those with left-wing politics. Churchgoing is declining particularly among the young. Thus the non-churchgoers in the 18–24-year-old age group amounted to 60% in Great Britain and France, 50% in Belgium, 45% in Denmark and Spain and 40% in the Netherlands. Since many young people never have prayers at home, the only place where they get any information about belief and church is religious instruction in school (if it exists). Here there are great challenges for the so-called 're-evangelization' of Europe.

We should note in passing that the great shortage of priests in a number of Western and Eastern European countries is an indicator of the shift in church allegiance in Europe.[5] The number of parishes without a resident priest is increasing rapidly (in West Germany now already 29%, in Switzerland 10%). In France, between 1977 and 1987 the (minimum) number increased from 1138 to 2754. In the Netherlands the number of priests engaged in pastoral work declined from 3,695 in 1960 to 1,842 in 1985. The aging of the clergy is felt increasingly strongly in Belgium, Austria, Great Britain and Italy, where the number of parishes without resident priests is steadily increasing. The long persecution of the church in Czechoslovakia and Hungary has meant that in both countries most of the priests, who are old, look after several parishes. Fortunately the number of pastorally committed laity has been steadily increasing in the meantime.

## 4. Church allegiance and ethics

From what I have said it is clear that there is already a distancing of church allegiance from ethics. Ethics is becoming autonomous. Between 1981 and 1990 permissiveness on the ethical level has increased. The EVSSG survey shows that opinions, even of practising Christians, on divorce, euthanasia, abortion and justice are becoming more tolerant. In all countries, including Poland, the majority approve of abortion where the mother's life is in danger or where a physically handicapped child is expected. The majority of the younger generation tolerate divorce and euthanasia; they see no difficulty in a woman having a child without a permanent relationship with a man. All in all opinion seems to be stricter over injustice than over what is permissible in the secular sphere.

No one would venture any predictions about the future religious development of Europe. There are no criteria for comparing religion in Europe with religion in other cultures. However, the present trends all point in one direction: the number of practising Christians is decreasing, and those who continue are increasingly adopting a selective attitude to what is officially offered or frowned on by the churches. The gap between church and world is increasing: younger people and women – without whom there can be no future – are increasingly critical of the institutional church. But people continue to seek spiritual help. In the meantime many people outside the churches have come to look for meaning. At the same time, the role of secular Europe is becoming increasingly important on the world stage. Only an 'evangelization' which tackles all these challenges and is prepared to meet them with dialogue has any chance of success. For the time being, the most creative spirits will have to come to terms with living in what Karl Rahner called a 'wintry period'.

*Translated by John Bowden*

## Notes

1. The Foundation is based in Amsterdam and the Secretariat is at the University of Tilburg, Netherlands. For information about the 1981 survey see J. Stoetzel, *Les valeurs du temps présent: un enquête européenne*, Paris 1983; S. Harding and

D. Phillips, *Contrasting Values in Western Europe*, London 1986; E. Noelle-Neumann and R. Köcher, *Die verletzte Nation*, Stuttgart 1987; L. Halman, F. Heunks, R. de Moor and H. Zanders, *Traditie, secularisatie en individualisering*, Tilburg 1987. The investigation was based on thousands of interviews in the countries concerned. The results of the 1990–1991 survey will be published in 1992 in both European syntheses and national analyses. At the time of writing (July 1991) the Spanish volume has already appeared: F. Orizo, *Los nuevos valores de los españoles*, Madrid 1991. The whole investigation in North America and Eastern and Western Europe covers about 800 million people above the age of eighteen.

2. Europe* includes the following countries: Belgium, France, West Germany, Great Britain, Ireland, Northern Ireland, Italy, the Netherlands, Portugal and Spain.

3. At the time of writing the investigation in Eastern Europe (including Czechoslovakia), is still in process.

4. See L. Halman, *Waarden in de Westerse Wereld*, Tilburg 1991.

5. A European survey of parishes without priests is in preparation.

# III · Quests

# The New Europe – A Challenge for the Churches

## Jacques Gaillot

The stability of Europe, which for forty years has stood between the two superpowers, has come to an end within a few months. The destruction of the Berlin wall, the reunification of Germany, the crumbling of the Marxist regimes in the majority of the Eastern countries, the profound reforms in the USSR, have suddenly given the old continent another face. After the hours of enthusiasm and joy which followed these events, the time has come to find a new balance. It is clear, for example, that the Europe of 1992 will not be that envisaged by the Common Market countries.

How is the church, how are the churches going to face the challenges of these profound changes within a changing Europe? Numerous Christians have been active in these transformations. However, that is already history. We now need to look forward to the future.

The few reflections which follow, coming as they do from a Catholic bishop, above all reflect the perspective of his church, but many of the remarks apply to all Christians, no matter to what church they belong, since they are concerned with the proclamation of the gospel.

## 1. Being the church in present-day Europe

In the near future the Catholic Church plans to convene a synod of bishops from all the countries of Europe, East and West, with observers from other Christian confessions, to take stock of the situation and identify directions for the future. The pope has already asked several times whether the church, while being and remaining what it is, is capable of facing a number of challenges posed by the modern world, like the future of young people, solidarity with the outcast and the risk of a two-speed society, secularization, dialogue with other religions.

To give a positive answer to these questions it is necessary to identify the many challenges posed by a Europe in the full flood of development, to shape attitudes and above all to plan for changes.

### (a)  Two indispensable attitudes

Many surveys of public opinion, especially among the young, indicate that Europeans have little interest in the churches and their declarations. In general they do not hear the good news that they expect from the churches. On the contrary, they hear many severe judgments and condemnations. Europe, they hear the churches saying, has betrayed its mission, lost many of the values which it formerly handed down, as a result of permissiveness. Europe is experiencing not only great indifference to faith, but also the loss of a sense of morality and traditions. This 'malign' attitude is contrary to the proclamation of the good news and should give way to what Paul VI advised in 1966: 'The Church must look on the world very much as God himself, after creation, looked on his marvellous and immense work, with an immense admiration, with great respect, with maternal sympathy and a generous love.' Christians are called to look on Europe and its development with very great good will.

In an article which appeared in *La Croix* on 29 November 1988, the philosopher René Remond noted another negative tendency in the church: 'It must be recognized that within the conciliar church one can note a tendency which without being integrist is integralist. There are those who are dreaming of recreating a Catholic society . . . It cannot be denied that many people are nostalgic for the Christianity of the old Europe. That is not the way forward. There is a need resolutely to find another way for the church to be present within a modern society which is developed and increasingly secularized.' That is not the way forward. A new page needs to be written; a positive attitude needs to be found.

### (b)  New ways

We must pursue these ways in the light of the Second Vatican Council, which called on Christians to share in 'the joy and hope, the grief and anguish of the men of our time, especially of those who are poor and afflicted in any way' (*Gaudium et Spes*, 1). These ways must be traced through the concerns and questions which are emerging in Europe today. The churches must involve themselves with everyone in order to find answers to the new problems which modern societies are posing every day. All the spheres of human activity have become building sites. After some decades of rapid development, the economy is now obviously in crisis and an important part of the population is feeling the effects. People have started talking about a two-speed society and have become resigned to the marginalization of the many people who no longer have food, purchasing power, good health. Scientific research and the constant invention of new technologies are rapidly transforming life and social structures. Everyone has to mobilize themselves to master these means so that all can benefit from them. How are we to react to biological research which raises so many specific and everyday questions for men and women, married couples and families? Again, computers are proving incredibly effective instruments, but they must be used for the service of human beings and not for a new concentration of power. Today everything is becoming an urgent question for tomorrow. Christians must be around where these questions are being raised, so that they can participate in the debates within society which will shed light and show ways forward. The gospel requires believers to commit themselves to the service of their fellow men and women, and especially those who at present are victims of a society which is changing and out of balance. This commitment often becomes a struggle to prevent fatalism in the face of inescapable economic necessities. If these necessities are not to become established as the norm, habits of selection and elimination are needed.

I want to cite one particular example, the struggle for peace. This is a point on which Christians should be unanimous, in the name of the gospel. Anything that puts peace in danger is now the business of all the inhabitants of the planet, even Europeans, who think that they have avoided all conflict for ever. But when I think of peace, I constantly ask myself about the scandal of the churches, which are still divided and sometimes in open conflict. Here is a challenge to face. What has happened to ecumenism after twenty years? Everyone says that it is in decline. Recently a student in a thesis wrote of religions as divisive factors . . .

Unless the churches present themselves to the world as workers for peace, who will believe them? What light will they be in the midst of our world? It is not enough to call down blessings on a unified Europe; if Europe is to be called on to show solidarity with other nations, there is a need to indicate the way to be taken. Europe is moving towards unity, and only the Christian churches remain divided. We must hope that the attempts at dialogue between Protestants and Catholics now beginning in Ireland will be the dawn of a new day.

Understanding between the churches will probably come about more rapidly if they mobilize at all levels to put themselves at the service of all men and women by taking specific objectives: solidarity, social planning, the fight against the scourges which destroy human life, like alcohol, drugs, guns and knives.

## 2. A constant conversion

If Christians aim to go alongside others on the way to the future they will constantly be led to ask themselves how faithful they are to the gospel and how their churches are living out what they commend and rejecting what they denounce.

### (a) Faithful to the gospel

The Council led the Catholic Church to discover its deep roots in the gospel. In this light the churches are constantly redefining themselves. The Council stressed two words which must characterize a church: 'servant' and 'poor'. Here we have the two constants in a call to conversion, a profound change which must come about at a deeper level than that of words. In all that is on the move and seeking a future in Europe, in the crises which are shaking societies, the churches are often caught in the act of giving priority to themselves, their place and their influence in society, not to mention, sometimes, their advantages and their privileges.

However, it is clear that the church will really be able to take part in the debates within society only if it has no other desire than to serve the human cause in an utterly disinterested way. It has to lose any pretensions to having answers in advance to all the questions which human beings face within the modern world. Nor must it propose solutions which are not completely disinterested. Here I am thinking of the recent negotiations in France over school timetables, and earlier over the status of private schools. In a debate on schools a church should have only one concern, an evangelical concern to put itself at the service of the poorest.

The challenge posed to the churches by the majority of the countries of Europe is that they should become truly lay. Instead of deploring the increasing secularization of societies, the church should recognize it as a normal development and call for a distinctive way of relating to it. This implies conversion to the acceptance of a loss of power, to being stripped down and having less influence. However, one condition is attached to that: a church must be able to speak a prophetic word in the present-day world. If it were no longer compromised by any power, the church would have the freedom to venture courageous statements on human and social questions. It could denounce inequalities, injustices, abuses of power, bearing witness by the way in which it functions itself.

## (b) Constant reform

Any standpoint, any denunciation, implies self-examination. It has to be logical. The church must itself do what it approves and reject what it condemns. Here a society like Europe poses many challenges to the church. The churches give their blessing to a growing Europe, rejoice at seeing the dividing walls crumble, the Soviet Union change its attitude and its ideology. But over this period have the churches themselves become places of real cooperation and communication? Is there the equivalent in the churches to the relationships which are being created everywhere at political, economic and cultural levels? Do not the churches remain very 'national'? Once again, it is amazing that the structure of a European church was not set up immediately after the Council. What is a fact in Latin America and Asia, and a desire in Africa, has yet to be realized in Europe. People are content with personal and occasional links, with *ad hoc* delegations. But nothing has really been set up to take account of the new Europe, its questions, its future. Who would be better placed than the church to provide a place for meeting, cooperation and reflection? Will the European Synod announced for 1992 be able to overcome this handicap? What will be the agenda? Will human questions or the questions of the church have the priority? It seems that a great many preoccupations are preventing the church from getting beyond the level of local and national churches, if only because of the differences which exist between these.

The churches are now rejoicing at the establishment of democratic regimes, especially in Eastern Europe. The end of the domination of the parties is hailed as real progress. It can be said that the whole of Europe is in the process of achieving true democracy. Within a society in which debates are public, decisions are arrived at by votes, and in which individuals have an increasing share in the decision-making, some churches maintain a monarchical-type system in which decisions are always taken at the top, in which powers are still markedly centralized, in which the choice of officials is made by the prince, and in which there is a permanent control on thought, morality and practice. How long will these anachronisms go on? There is also an urgent need for conversion here. What is said to be good for civil societies must also be good for the churches. For some years now, Christians have at last come to view the 'Declaration on Human Rights', the basis of the dominant political and social regimes in Europe, as progress and as a benefit for men and women. That has not always been the case, and since the 'rights of man' and the 'Enlightenment' were both condemned by Pius VI at the time of the French Revolution, they have been rejected and scorned by the church. So approval and defence of them marks some advance. But they also constitute a challenge, since it is not certain that these rights are always respected by the churches themselves. It would also be good also to check the way in which the co-responsibility of which there is so much talk is exercised. For example, in 1972 the bishops of France published a text 'All Responsible in the Church'. This pioneered the way and made it possible to advance with confidence along a new road. What has happened to that today, after twenty years? Who are really responsible? Has the exercise of power really been devolved in the church? Within a modern society it is important for the members of the people of God and especially lay people to achieve a real sharing of responsibility, a real participation in decision-making, and greater freedom of speech.

## 3. Planetary dimensions

### (a) The Third World still exists

If the churches want to speak a prophetic word today in a Europe which is in process of construction and reconstruction, they must vigorously denounce the way in which the Third World is in process of sinking into oblivion. The attention of Europeans has been distracted from countries which are either developing or in an economic recession. All efforts are being concentrated on the reunification of East and West and its consequences.

Aid to the Eastern countries is legitimate and indispensable, but it must not obscure the dramatic reality of the situation in the rest of the world. Europe risks becoming shut in on itself, obsessed with the possibilities of a new market and new investments. Many people are dreaming of the creation of a powerful bloc over against North America and alongside the remnants of Soviet power. This bloc would involve only a few hundred million inhabitants. How far is it still listening to the appeals from the South Americans, Africans and other countries of the world, which are in grave difficulty? Who will be the voice of the poor in the midst of the wealthy if not the churches, in the name of the gospel?

Instead of blessing the coming into being of this powerful Europe or dreaming of the restoration of the old Christendom, the churches are challenged to remind the old Europe that it cannot abandon solidarity with the rest of the world, that it must mobilize itself again for the just development of all peoples. It is not a matter of offering voluntary help in time of catastrophe, but of justice. It is a matter of life and death for Europe itself, since this international solidarity will help it to find its own way and its own health. If it formed itself into a rich and separate bloc, the Europe of 1992 would risk being choked with consumerism and using up all its energies in economic competition and new cold wars.

The churches must take the risk of arousing public opinion on such serious issues as armaments and arms dealing, which divert immense resource that otherwise would allow all human beings to share in true economic growth and just development. This is a particularly important question for Europe, since the enormous military forces which were thought indispensable because of the tension between East and West are no longer justified.

### (b)  The challenge of the Fourth World

Along the same lines, in making themselves once again the voice of the poor, the churches must say clearly that certain features of the Third World are also appearing today in the most advanced industrialized countries of Europe. The very rapid development of technologies, of modes of production, of trade and consumption, are forcing more and more men and women to the periphery of society. Those who are weakest, of least use, least adaptable, are eliminated, and form what has come to be called the Fourth World. The churches must fight to ensure that human beings are not regarded as merchandise, and to recall, in the words of John Paul II in his last encyclical, that some things are due to human beings precisely because they are human beings.

It is impossible not to mention here the challenge posed by the advent and presence of immigrants from all over the world in most European countries. They too are often thought of as merchandise, as a labour force for the most menial tasks. They get a poor welcome, little acceptance, are barely integrated and increasingly rejected, though no one would be willing to replace them in the work they do. It is worth speaking out clearly in the name of sheer common sense: whether we like it or not, numerous poor people are invading our rich and underpopulated countries. It is urgent for the churches to speak out on behalf of a politics of integration at every level of society. We all know that this is not easy. Encounter between religions which have old unsettled accounts is not the least difficulty. The churches have had twenty-five years to create the conditions for encounter which the Council wanted. As the Declaration on non-Christian Religions put it: 'There is no basis either in theory or in practice for any discrimination between individual and individual, or between people and people, arising either from human dignity or from the rights which flow from it' (no. 5). In the name of the gospel, Christians must do everything possible to ensure that this dignity and these rights of so many of their brothers and sisters are respected.

## 4. Listening to other continents

The churches, which are present on all the continents, represent an opportunity for the human future. Provided that real communication exists between these churches, each of them, by virtue of their roots in different countries and cultures, has an original experience, an indispensable contribution, to make to building a human future.

The church of Europe has every interest in listening to its younger sisters. Too often it plays the part of the mother, not to say the grandmother, who claims to know everything and seeks to control everything. But how many new dynamisms, how many original discoveries in the churches of other continents, could the churches of Europe use to their benefit?

One thinks immediately of the church of the poor in Latin America. We can learn from this how any new evangelization can come about only through the situation of the outcast and the suffering. This church is tracing out a new and vital way through the birth of church base communities. It is teaching us all that there is no good news without a concrete struggle against all that wounds, oppresses and kills people.

The African churches can help us to face the challenge of the absence of brotherhood among the peoples. Those who have had the experience of so much humiliation, oppression, exploitation, deportation and scorn are claiming a place among all peoples as brothers and sisters, in the name of the gospel. Here is a challenge to the churches to be places of real welcome and brotherhood.

The minority churches in Asia can remind us that the great religions are all Asiatic. Buddha, Muhammad and Jesus were born on this continent. These churches know that no evangelization is possible without first entering into profound friendship, esteem and collaboration. What opportunities there are for our churches to welcome so much richness! What challenges there are for the churches of Europe!

Furthermore, many Christians from other continents look to their European brothers for an original statement, an attitude which will help them to live better. All people, rich or poor, are on the eve of entering, or have already entered, the modern world. Industry and its technologies can now be found all over the world; the media diffuse information and convey cultures; the universities train young people in every aspect of modern knowledge. All these people are calling on old Europe to help them, by means of its own experience, to find new ways. Many are disappointed at our silence and our slackness. There is a new challenge, which is no less than universal, to allow men and women to enter the modern world, to have a positive experience of secularization.

What will the churches of Europe say and do? What good news will they bring in words and actions to this Europe which is in process of construction and which is seeking a new unity? What encouragement will they give to all those moving towards peace, justice and solidarity? What denunciation of everything that causes regression, imprisonment, marginalization?

The churches must give a generous welcome to this world which is coming into being, with its riches and its ambiguities. This welcome cannot but renew the churches themselves. Going along with men and women on the way towards their future will transform the churches. It will make them, too, capable of newness, of renewal, of the discovery of creation.

*Translated by John Bowden*

# Freedom in Solidarity – The Rescue of Reason

## Johann Baptist Metz

### 1. The two sides of the European spirit

*'Eurocentrism'?*

'Eurocentrism' is the main charge continually levelled against the European spirit, in the wider world and in Europe itself, especially today. The Europeans are constantly criticized for being too Euro-centric. But what does 'Eurocentric' mean? Where is the Eurocentrism of the European spirit rooted? My answer is brief and to the point: it is rooted, not in the fact that we Europeans have 'exported' too much of Europe to the world, but in the fact that we have exported too little, or, more precisely, that we have always sought to disseminate only half of Europe, half of the European spirit throughout the world. I know that this answer sounds provocative, and is open to possible misunderstand-ings, but I hope that it will take on clearer contours in the remarks which follow.

*European rationality – type I*

By means of science and technology, or the so-called technological civilization, Europe has to some degree come to dominate the world and thus has created the one world which we now experience, with all its contradictions, open and latent. With its information and communications industry it moves like a bulldozer all over the globe. Everywhere brains are being Europeanized as a result of this technical modernization. So-called occidental rationality is bringing about the secular Europeanizing of the world. As is well known, this type of rationality, which has its roots in Europe, is governed by a will to power over untamed nature. Its knowledge is a form of the knowledge for ruling. The logic inherent in it is a logic of domination, not of recognition; it is at any rate a logic of assimilation and transformation, not a logic of otherness.

## European rationality – type II

But is the message of the European spirit exhausted in this secular Europeanizing of the world? If the answer is yes, what might the consequences be? In the course of this secular Europeanizing, would not all other cultures increasingly be marginalized and turned into folk-lore? Would not their alien prophecies ultimately fall silent – even and particularly for Europeans themselves? A new type of rationality is developing, above all in the processes of the European Enlightenment. It is directed by a reason which wants to be become effective and achieve itself as freedom – also and specifically as the freedom of others, and thus as justice. This type of rationality is the basis for a new political culture which has in view the subjective freedom and worth of all human beings. This universal message, which is native to the European spirit, is strictly anti-Eurocentric. Without its dissemination throughout the world, the secular Europeanizing of the world would be simply a contribution to its downfall. Not all universalism is an expression of the will to power. Certainly this kind of 'European universalism', this 'universalism of human rights' (as one might well also call it), can only come about if it is disseminated in a readiness to recognize the otherness of others, i.e. only if the age of European insensitivity which has already cost so many victims is not repeated in the age of human rights.

## 2. The crisis

But what about this 'good' and promising half of the European spirit in Europe itself? In answering this question we should not be too self-confident, too uncritical. Here we will do well to resort to a bit of ideological criticism, an approach which seems little heeded or even neglected today. Here I would mention just one prominent instance of the currently all too self-confident and uncritical approach to the basic European situation – and I see that situation not only in continental Europe but in North America as well. In summer 1989 an article appeared in the USA entitled 'The End of History?'. It was written by Francis Fukuyama, head of the planning staff in the State Department. Briefly, Fukuyama's thesis is that the West has now finally won the Cold War and therefore the United States has become the apotheosis of everything that was to be expected in history from Western European modernity. Does this completely ignore the dangers inherent in the West, in the European spirit? It seems to me particularly important to point to them in view of the fundamental changes in Europe, the 'new Europe'. Has it been demonstrated, for example, that the type of rationality which is stamped by the will to power, the type of reality which believes it can do anything, has not also swallowed up the type of reality which I described as a type of reason seeking culture and justice, and thus as the basis for a new political culture? Is there not a danger that the 'good' European spirit only acts as compensation, and has no substance? In Europe, too, the so-called processes of modernization are increasingly running by themselves, with no subjective control over them. What about this 'good' spirit of Europe? Let me mention some symptoms of its crisis or its threatening collapse – and I hope that I can do this without being too pessimistic about our culture.

## Technology and the information industry

There is such a thing as the death of the freedom-seeking spirit, extrapolated by technology. A freedom based on the subject and on solidarity seems long since to have been overdetermined by technology. Increasingly we have techniques for reproducing everything, ultimately even reproducing human beings who themselves reproduce. Human beings are increasingly just their own experiment and less and less their own memory. Has not the model long been a computerized intelligence which cannot remember itself because it also cannot forget anything, in other words an intelligence without history, without passion and without morality?

Is this development aimed at heightened independence or does it lead to a new, to some degree secondary, bondage, a bondage which is far harder to overcome than the first bondage at the time of the Enlightenment because those who are the victims of secondary bondage do not even suffer as a result of the bondage in which they suffer? How compatible with the media and with sources of information is that spirit in search of itself, as the freedom of the subject in solidarity? In recent years North American scientists in particular have pointed to the ambiguities in our modern culture and information industry. The mass media do not just result in richer subjectivity with more intense perception; they also encourage a kind of lassitude in the subject, by making increasingly unnecessary the effort of creating language which we have imagined ourselves and history which we have experienced ourselves. The flood of information apparently serves not only to enlighten, but also to some degree to bring a new secondary form of bondage, because it increasingly detaches people from the possibilities and even the consequences of their concrete actions. So is the spirit of European modernity, the spirit of the Enlightenment, slowly but surely turning into a second bondage?

*Scientific theory*

There is such a thing as the death of the freedom-seeking type of rationality, extrapolated by scientific theory. At the moment our modern scientific knowledge is not orientated on the subject as the basis of knowledge. 'Subject', and also 'freedom', 'liberation', and so on are, in strict scientific terms, anthropomorphisms. In terms of scientific theory, if I understand it rightly, talk of freedom of the subject in solidarity is an anachronism. To know what is the case one has to begin from the death of the subject. There are no subjects, only self-referential systems. The spontaneity of the spirit does not rule in them. That would be an idea left over from the 'old Europe'. Rather, what rules is the coldness of space, the coldness of an infinitely indifferent evolution, a history of evolution without a subject.

*Neomyths*

In my view, the new delight in myths which is springing up, the neomythic cult of European postmodernity, points to the death of that type of rationality which seeks expression in the freedom of the subject in solidarity. In the farewell to European modernity which is so often celebrated, a new cult is being disseminated, a cult of shedding obligations, a new cult of innocence, praise of myth because of the ethical suspension which it contains, because of the supposition of human innocence which is grounded in it. Now only qualified options are available. Commitment, if there is any, is commitment with the right of exchange: 'Here I stand, but I can also do other things. I am never merely my own opinion. Anything goes, including the opposite.'

As we know, in the background here we have Nietzsche, the prophet of farewell to European modernity. However, we should note that this Nietzsche is not just the herald of the death of God in the heart of Europe, the passionate critic of Christian 'monotono-theism' in favour of a Dionysian polymythy, but also the herald of the death of human beings as we have so far known and been familiar with them. As is well known, Nietzsche himself speaks of the death of the subject; he regards the subject as a mere 'fiction', and talk of 'I' as an anthropomorphism. He already describes the collapse of truth-seeking language in the intoxication of metaphors and subject-less discourse. He prophesies and calls for the end of normative-moral consciousness in a life 'beyond good and evil' in which the successor to man, super-elevated man, is none other than his own infinite experiment. Certainly – for the sake of Nietzsche – we ought to differentiate more closely here. However, I am simply challenging the stereotype which Nietzsche himself comes across as. Does his 'new man', the exalted Dionysian man, reflect the future of the European spirit? A freedom 'beyond good and evil', remote from memory, suffering and mourning, above all an innocent freedom? This self-realization of the European spirit in a Dionysian mode is not necessarily utopian. Its most trivial realization is obvious: human beings as gently functioning machines.

### 3. Safeguarding theological traces

It may be that I have exaggerated this crisis of the European spirit. I will not deny a degree of one-sidedness. It may be useful in due course to seek correctives. Are there any? Be this as it may, many people nowadays are in search of such correctives, as resources for resistance. They turn directly to cultures outside Europe and their wisdoms.

Here I would like to suggest taking note of the depths of European culture itself – in particular where they go back to the biblical traditions. From them it is possible to derive themes for the spirit and culture of a freedom in solidarity which seem to me indispensable in the situation of crisis that I have described. Certainly these motives and perspectives have been obscured, not least by the way in which Christianity became theology. That makes all the more urgent the task of rescuing them from oblivion or even that oblivion of oblivion which prevails in theological discourse. What follows can be no more than a safeguarding of their traces in the crisis of the European spirit.

*Anamnetic rationality*

The kind of perception of the world which was at work in original Christianity takes the form of anamnetic reason. The type of rationality in the biblical traditions, if I may put it that way, is thus basically anamnetic. It resorts to the indissoluble unity of reason and memory – and precisely this seems to me to be repressed or forgotten in the Enlightenment type of rationality in search of freedom. There is good reason for the Enlightenment criticism of dogmatism and traditionalism. But has it not overlooked the fact that there is a particular form of memory in that critical reason which does not want to be pure criticism? Has it not overlooked the fact that not only faith but also that reason which seeks to be effective as freedom needs such memory? Over against the world of our scientific and technological systems this memory takes the form of a dangerous memory, a dangerous memory without which human beings increasingly lose themselves as subjects seeking freedom in solidarity. In remembering this, reason seeks to assure itself of the semantic content on which not only the substance of faith but also interest in subjective freedom and freedom in solidarity feeds. Now Christianity has indeed preserved the anamnetic character of its identity in worship ('Do this in remembrance of me'). But it has largely neglected to develop this anamnetic constitution culturally and to defend it against an abstract modern reason. Only where Christianity succeeds in doing that can it also enter into the crisis of the European spirit with saving criticism.

## A memory of God that is critical of myth

The European spirit as manifested in the processes of the Enlightenment sought above all to break out of the anxieties of a mythically bewitched world in the interest of human freedom. This concern also governed the radical Enlightenment criticism of religion. However, one question here cannot either be answered or excluded, namely the question of consolation. So the freedom-seeking spirit of the Enlightenment constantly produced new irrationalisms by suppressing this question – against its declared intent: new myths, say, as clandestine ways out of the straits of historical life, as ways of shedding the concrete experiences of suffering and catastrophe and of absorbing anxiety and guilt.

The memory of God in the biblical traditions is more radically aware than the Enlightenment type of rationality of a criticism of all myths, or at any rate of a proviso which is critical of myths. In the earliest biblical traditions the name 'God' was applied for the first time and uniquely in the history of humankind to human beings. Israel's capacity for God here is evidently rooted in a remarkable incapacity, namely the incapacity really to find comfort in myths or ideas remote from history. Biblical monotheism is accompanied by a pathos which is critical of myth. However, at present even Christian theology is often distancing itself from this monotheism. It is seeking, for example through depth psychology, to go behind it to a polymythic primal history of humankind or to see through it in trinitarian theology to a history within God. But in my view such attempts reflect a world with a mystical and polytheistic character which has lost the power to be critical of myth. The new praise of myth in the postmodern spirit of Europe makes me suspicious: is not the ethical suspension sought in myth, the assumption of a radical human innocence given by myth, a disguised form of despair at freedom, above all at thoughts of freedom in solidarity in the face of the injustice in our world which cries out to heaven?

### A culture of acknowledgment

The Enlightenment type of rationality on which our political culture in search of freedom and justice is based was always threatened by the dangers of ethnocentric and culturally monocentric short-cuts. Time and again, it seems, this new political culture came to grief on the others, whom it had to recognize and acknowledge in their otherness. In the face of this crisis I want to refer to a third impulse which is indebted to biblical traditions. Within them lies the impulse to a hermeneutical culture which acknowledges others in their otherness. The neighbours in the central biblical commandment to love the neighbour are not primarily those who are near, but the others, the alien others. Does Christianity still have the power to cultivate this biblical knowledge of the traces of God in the otherness of others? Only if it does, can it offer support in the crisis of the European spirit and its universalist morality. Certainly the idea of acknowledgment here is not aimed at transforming the others in their otherness. Nor is otherness in itself already a matter of being 'in the truth'. Otherwise everything would end up in a vague relativism of cultural worlds, a relativism already bearing within itself the germ of a new uncomprehended violence. Consequently the hermeneutical culture sought here may not abandon the tension between the authenticity of cultural worlds and the universalism of human rights developed in the European tradition. Nowadays there is almost everything still to be done in this direction, not only in politics but also in the church.

*Translated by John Bowden*

# Beyond Foundationalism and Relativism: Hermeneutics and the New Ecumenism

## David Tracy

### 1. Introduction: the New Europe and the old epistemology

That classic work of Western modernity, Edmund Husserl's *The Crisis of European Science*, is one of the last great texts of European intellectual self-confidence. But what a strange self-confidence Husserl possessed! On the one hand, Husserl insists that only a rigorous, apodictic form of phenomenology could save the 'scientific' character of Western thought. On the other hand, Husserl argues – and here is the classic note of tragedy, that peculiar and extraordinary product of Western sensibility – that without such scientific rigour, European thought and culture would become merely one more anthropological type. What a strange and hybristic thought! For Husserl, non-European cultures can be adequately studed by anthropology, that peculiarly Western discipline for understanding the non-European 'other'. One studies 'Europe', however, only through the discipline of history for its past and the discipline of 'social science' for its present. But one would never study 'Europe' through anthropology – that is a discipline designed to help 'us' understand 'them'.

The European theologians of modernity had their own form of a sane and noble but ultimately tragic Western hybris. Adolf von Harnack spoke for many in his period of modern European self-confidence when he insisted that it was not necessary to study 'other' religions – i.e., other than Christianity. For to understand Christianity for the historian-theologian von Harnack, after all, is to understand all religions. Some Christian theologians, of course, did attempt to understand 'other' religions in order to understand Christianity itself better – like Schleiermacher and Hegel before Harnack, like Troeltsch and von Hügel after him. But even these exceptional thinkers usually had either explicit (Hegel, Schleiermacher) or implicit (von Hügel, early Troeltsch) developmental schemata designed to show in good, modern, European fashion how European Christianity is, of course, the highest religion.

There are only a few European or non-European Christians who believe any longer in such developmental schemata, i.e., schemata with a secretly evolutionary sense of time and a culturally colonialist sense of space. The fact is that developmental notions are not the proper way to understand the relationship of Christianity to the other great religious traditions.[1] Indeed, more and more theologians, European as well as those in Africa, Asia, Oceania, and the Americas, now believe that all serious theology today will try to work out an adequate Christian theology only by trying to understand Christianity in culturally and politically non-Eurocentric ways. Perhaps only by trying to understand the meaning of the other great religions can a modern Christian achieve an appropriate Christian self-understanding in the late twentieth century. This latter 'new ecumenism', moreover, needs to be worked out from the beginning of a theology and at every crucial moment in theology. The question of the 'other religions' can no longer be left for an appendix to a theology.

The many new reflections, in Europe and by interested non-Europeans like myself, on the remarkable emergence in the global sense of a 'new Europe' may yet prove, paradoxically perhaps, a hopeful sign for all serious theology in a 'world church' and a global community. For the 'new Europe' clearly need not be a return of European hybris culturally, politically, or theologically. To be sure, some neo-conservative theologians with their talk of a 'Christian Europe' do sound disturbingly like Hilaire Belloc with his famous saying, 'Europe is the faith and the faith is Europe'. But even many neo-conservative Eurocentric theologians do seem to sense that the new Europe should not mean the return of Christendom. Something else is happening in these thoughts of a 'new Europe': a new modesty in celebrating difference and otherness amidst a new-found communality; a new experience of the vital traditions of self-criticism and ethical universalism of rights and justice, which 'Europe' also means throughout the world.

Perhaps, after all, the new Europe with its noble hope for an ethical communality amidst cultural and political differences may paradoxically mean the end of Eurocentrism – even in theology. Perhaps, after all, the new multi-religious and multi-cultural Europe may mean something very hopeful indeed. It may mean, first, the hope for a new kind of inter-religious ecumenism as part of all Christian theological self-consciousness.

Second, it may mean the hope for a new kind of cross-cultural enrichment within Europe with its remarkable cultural and religious differences. Consider, for example, the possible difference to French – and thereby European – theology when the new Muslim reality in France (indeed, throughout the new Europe) becomes a serious theological concern. Third, the new Europe may mean hope for a new kind of intellectual self-understanding where the brilliance and self-critical powers of European modes of thought can force European thought (including European theologies and philosophies) away from whatever remnants of Eurocentrism still remain in their self-understandings. The rest of the world looks once again to a post-colonialist Europe for new guidance for the cultural and religious ecumenism which all theology needs.

## 2.  The new hermeneutics as discourse analysis: from historical context to social location

Let us reflect on each of these new hopes, starting with the new forms of the classic self-critical power of European thought. The reign of epistemology has ended in European philosophy and theology. The belief of the great moderns from Descartes through Husserl that philosophy can secure some sure, certain, presuppositionless 'foundation' for all thought and thereby for all reality has collapsed. This peculiarly modern temptation – now named 'foundationalism' – is in widespread dispute. The alternative, alas, is too often some form of postmodern relativism, whether explicit or implicit, whether self-confident or modest.

Hermeneutics has been one major alternative to both foundationalism and relativism. Hermeneutics has managed to take 'historical context' with full seriousness and thereby abandoned foundationalism without yielding to relativism. It is hardly surprising that so much European thought of our period is either hermeneutical in origin (like deconstructionism) or hermeneutical in intent if not name (like the dialogical thought of Bakhtin and many forms of East European and Central European semiotics and structuralism). Almost all present forms of Continental European thought attempt to be in conversation with, and sometimes in conflict with, contemporary European hermeneutics as the major twentieth-century intellectual expression of post-foundationalist but non-relativist European thought. Especially when hermeneutics is allied (see Habermas, Apel, Ricoeur) with some form of critical theory or some form of the 'new pragmatism', the hope for intellectual position beyond both foundationalism and relativism is genuine.[2] But many modern hermeneutical thinkers now believe that hermeneutics should be reformulated in our period by shifting the traditional hermeneutical emphases from 'text' to 'discourse', from 'historical context' to 'social location'.

The shift from classical consciousness to historical consciousness, as Ernst Troeltsch and Bernard Lonergan argued in their distinct ways, was undoubtedly the major issue facing theology in the nineteenth and early twentieth centuries. Such historical consciousness, moreover, need not remain merely cultural and thereby idealist. Historical consciousness can also become (and has become, especially with the emergence of political, liberation and feminist theologies) both cultural and economic, social and political. The development of new practical theologies in our period, moreover, has encouraged the same set of moves: first, from the individualism and idealism of earlier existentialist, personalist and trans-cendental theologies and philosophies to a politically-oriented theology related to practical philosophies and to committed social, political and religious *praxis*; second, from the earlier purely cultural analyses of historical consciousness to analyses related to social, political and religious praxis.

In hermeneutical terms, this series of refinements of the meaning of historical consciousness and historicity had two principal consequences. First, there exists the widespread recovery of practical philosophies (such as Aristotelian notions of *phronesis*, virtue, and community; Hegelian and Marxist notions of praxis; the new North American and German pragmatism) as the necessary ally to hermeneutical theory. Second, there exist as post-Heideggerian and post-Gadamerian hermeneutics less purely culturalist notions of historicity. Indeed, the use of critical theory in Habermas as well as Ricoeur's development of a hermeneutics of suspicion (Freud, Marx, Nietzsche) to parallel Gadamer's earlier hermeneutics of retrieval may now justly be viewed as philosophical parallels to the emergence of political and practical theologies in our period.

To shift the language of hermeneutics from 'historical context' to 'social location' is simply to render yet more explicit the need for a hermeneutics of suspicion for every non-idealist philosophy and theology. All hermeneutics by definition take history seriously. All hermeneutics may also believe that a critique of conscious errors (encouraged by the hermeneutical model of conversation) is insufficient for all interpretive issues. But as political, liberation and feminist theologies have clearly demonstrated, our problems *with* history (the tradition) and *in* history (our present social, economic, political and ecclesial situation) are not confined to corrigible conscious errors (i.e., corrigible through better inquiry, better conversation, better argument, better hermeneutics of retrieval). Rather, our present problems include the need to suspect (the verb is accurate) that we are likely to find not merely conscious errors but also unconscious systemic illusions in all history, all tradition, all texts, all interpretations.

The language of 'social location' (as distinct from the earlier, simpler, and too often purely culturalist and idealist language of 'historical context') renders explicit this need for a hermeneutics of suspicion for all adequate interpretation. For to speak of the need to analyse 'social location' is to insist on the need for explicit attention to gender, race and class issues in all theological interpretation and all hermeneutics.

Any emphasis on social location can be properly viewed as a development of hermeneutics rather than a replacement of hermeneutics. On one count, however, hermeneutics itself must change: viz., by shifting its own emphasis from 'text' to 'discourse'.[3] The focus on text in modern hermeneutics has become dangerous not only for its privileging of literate over pre-literate cultures (the latter often revealingly labelled 'pre-historical'), but also for the idealist and purely culturalist assumptions of the category 'text'. 'Discourse', on the other hand, always demands attention to explicit or implicit power realities in the emergence of meaning and knowledge. For discourse not only means (as in Benveniste) 'someone says something to someone' but also demands attention to forms of power operative in the someone, the something, the 'to someone'. Discourse analysis should not reduce meaning and knowledge to power relations. But discourse analysis also will not allow (as earlier forms of historical consciousness and hermeneutics could allow) an abstraction from the specific realities of power, especially the relationships of gender, class, and race: in all texts, all tradition, all interpretation and all knowledge – and thereby in all theology.

In so far as a hermeneutics of suspicion expands beyond the earlier psychoanalytical and revisionary Marxist models of the early Frankfurt school to some form of discourse analysis that deals with gender, race and class issues (and preferably all three issues systemically related), then modern hermeneutical theology becomes yet more practical and ethical-political without ceasing to be fundamentally hermeneutical. For any form of discourse analysis that abandons its hermeneutical origins is likely to become either foundationalist (i.e., purely ideological) or implicitly relativist (as in much of Foucault and Foucault-inspired discourse analysis).

All hermeneutical forms of discourse analysis are (as liberation and feminist theologies implictly are; as many other forms of practical theology explicitly are) neither foundationalist nor relativist in character. Liberation theology, for example, is, by its very emphasis on social-economic-political context, clearly non-foundationalist. At the same time, all forms of liberation theology correctly insist upon the implicit universality of the liberationist ethical appeal to justice. They are, therefore, not relativist, for justice, however rooted in context, must be universal or it cannot be just. The move, therefore, past a hermeneutical overconcern with 'text' and 'historical context' into a new hermeneutical concern with 'social location' and 'discourse' can be construed as a self-critical move within the non-foundationalist and non-relativist horizon of modern European hermeneutics. Only when discourse analysis becomes either foundationalist (ideological) or relativist does it become anti-hermeneutical. Hermeneutics, thus reconstrued as hermeneutical discourse analysis, continues to seem the most representative form of European thought concerned to move beyond foundationalism and relativism.

### 3. The new ecumenism: Christian theology and the discovery of the other

The new Europe as a new world church also clearly calls for a new spiritual journey by all Christian theologians: into a new ecumenism where the other religious traditions become central to genuine Christian self-understanding; where the issue of the 'other' becomes central to intra-European and global awareness. This inter-religious consciousness first emerged in the non-European cultures of the new Asian and African Christian theologies; then in the rediscovery of indigenous traditions in the theologies of the Americas (especially African-American theologies in North America and the debate on 'popular religion' in Latin America); that consciousness has now come full circle into the new inter-religious consciousness of European culture.

Many spiritual journeys are like the classic European journey of Ulysses: one wanders far and long but eventually returns home. However bad the trespassers who have usurped the old place, most at home remember one fondly; most even realize that one had to leave for a while; most do not demand an explanation. The journey of any Christian theology aware of the impact of other religions is a different one from the classical models for Western Christian odysseys. In the new Europe, as elsewhere, there is a new form of spiritual journey, new for Christianity and for all traditions in this late twentieth century. The new search is likely to become that of more and more religious persons: stay faithful to your own tradition; go deeper and deeper into its particularities; defend and clarify its identity. At the same time, wander, Ulysses-like, willingly, even eagerly, among other great traditions and ways; try to learn something of their beauty and truth;

concentrate on their otherness and difference as the new route to communality.[4]

On the one hand, the new ecumenism agrees with the heart of all the classic religious journeys: the universal is to be found by embracing the particular. Indeed, those who break through to a universal religious message are always highly particular in both origin and expression. Surely this route through the particular is a wiser way to find truth than seeking that ever-elusive goal, a common denominator among the religions. Some people can speak Esperanto. Most of us would rather learn Spanish or Chinese or Arabic or English.

On the other hand, all religious thinkers today, while remaining faithful to the particular religious traditions which have nourished us with the spiritual truths through which we actually see and feel the world, should find new ways to learn from the other traditions. There are, to be sure, many religious thinkers who find it necessary to stay solely on one way, one path, one journey, one exclusive path to God – and give no attention to other ways. These same persons have their own Belloc-like versions of Europe as Christendom. There are still others who believe, sometimes seriously (as in Gandhi and John Hick), sometimes lazily, that all the great ways are merely different expressions of the same truth and the same goal; for example, from self-centredness to Reality-centredness.'[5] The new ecumenism impelled by the new Europe is in search of some third way: you may find yourself and the truth of your tradition's way best by being grounded in self-respect while still exposing yourself fully to other ways, other journeys, other traditions. Near the end of his life, for example, Thomas Merton learned Zen practices and began to call himself a 'self-transcending Christian'. A similar leitmotif occurs through the interest in other religions among many theologians today who (directly contrary to von Harnack) believe that to understand even one's own tradition well, one must understand several traditions. Anyone who undertakes this journey must try to hold together three virtues ordinarily kept apart: the virtue of self-respect and self-dignity maintained by all those who never leave their tradition; the virtue of a radical openness to other and different traditions; the virtue of ethical universality with a sense of justice by all who insist upon the communality of the human. But what can the 'new Europe' mean without that threefold sense of self-respect, openness to difference and otherness, and the ethical universality of true and liberating justice?

Today such new choices in Europe throughout the globe are clearly necessary ones. For once any of us learns that we are in a tradition (cultural or religious), we can no longer be in that tradition the way we once were. Our choices then become stark: retrenchment (enter fundamentalism);

flight (enter relativism); or what Paul Ricoeur nicely named a 'second naiveté' towards one's tradition (enter critical philosophy and revisionary theology) allied to a genuine openness to otherness and difference. Ulysses-like, theologians need to wander: through modern critical approaches; through an exposure to other ways – religious, non-religious, anti-religious. For many contemporary persons, there is no longer the possibility of a first naiveté towards one's own tradition and cultural home. The only serious question becomes: is a second naiveté possible? If so, how? Any of us may rediscover our traditions, i.e., experience a second naiveté towards its beauty and its truth, in and through discovering others, their difference, and their truth. But is it possible to honor the truth of one's own religious tradition while being genuinely open to other great ways as other? Clearly, the answer must be yes, or we are all lost in a Hobbesian state of the war of all against all.

The theological alternative is clear: a fidelity to the ever-greater God in a new cultural and religious situation where the realities of otherness and difference are critically and religiously appropriated by all Christian theologies that dare to move beyond any form of intellectual foundationalism and its institutional counterparts, cultural imperialism and ecclesial triumphalism, and beyond any exhausted model of liberal modernity that can promise only relativism. The emerging world church is newly anxious to be freed of Eurocentrism – freed above all by the theologies of the new Europe that struggles to find a new inter-cultural and inter-religious theological identity for itself. Once again the theological world turns to Europe for new, non-Eurocentric guidance and new, non-foundationalist and non-relativist, hope. European hermeneutics reconstrued as hermeneutical discourse analysis shows the way forward intellectually. Will the new European theologies show the same hermeneutical and political way forward in an increasingly multi-cultural, multi-religious and yet unifying world of common meanings for justice, by listening to the oppressed and marginalized – and for theo-logical hope in the ever greater God?

## Notes

1. See Hans Küng, Josef von Ess, Heinrich von Stietencron, Heinz Bechert, *Christianity and the World Religions*, London and New York 1985.
2. See Richard J. Bernstein, *Beyond Objectivism and Relativism: Science, Hermeneutics and Praxis*, Philadelphia 1983; Richard Hollinger (ed.), *Hermeneutics and Praxis*, Notra Dame, Ind. 1985; Price R. Wachterhauser (ed.), *Hermeneutics and Modern Philosophy*, Albany, New York 1986.

3. On 'text', see the ground-breaking study of Werner G. Jeanrond, *Text and Interpretation as Categories of Theological Thinking*, New York 1988.

4. For two expressions of this attempt, see John Cobb, *Beyond Dialogue: Toward a Mutual Transformation of Christianity and Buddhism*, Philadelphia 1982; David Tracy, *Dialogue with the Other: The Inter-Religious Dialogue*, Louvain 1990.

5. See John Hick, *An Interpretation of Religion: Human Responses to the Transcendent*, New Haven and London 1989.

# The Commitment of the Conciliar Process

## Marga Bührig

### The history of the term 'conciliar process'

At its Sixth General Assembly in Vancouver in 1983 the World Council of Churches (WCC) formulated as its task for the next seven years: 'A focal point of the WCC programme will be to bind the member churches to a conciliar process of mutual commitment (covenant) for justice, peace and the preservation of the whole creation. The basis of this focus will be the confession of Jesus Christ as the life of the world and Christian resistance against the demonic powers of death in racism, sexism, economic exploitation, militarism and the misuse of science and technology.'[1] The programme was backed up by a 'Public Declaration on Peace and Justice' which contained a wealth of specific suggestions. The description I have just given contains the terms which appear in the title of this article: conciliar process, commitment (further strengthened by the verb 'bind'), and then as a further definition of the commitment the word 'covenant' in brackets. At a glance it is clear that this is not just the announcement of a new study theme. The aim was shared commitment of the member churches to an act of surrender and trust in the face of the threats to justice, peace and the whole creation.

On closer inspection, the combination of these terms seems less clear. WCC documents were already speaking of conciliar fellowship in the late 1960s. The church was to be seen as a conciliar fellowship of local churches. This was deliberately understood as the way to a universal council or a transition to a council which was not possible then (and is still not possible now). The idea of the unity of the churches plays a major part in this concept.

Since Vancouver it has been associated with the mutual commitment of the churches to justice, peace and the integrity of creation. In the German-language area the significance of 'conciliar' has further been accentuated by the call of the scientist and peace researcher Friedrich von Weizsäcker for a Council of Peace, a call which surprised the German Evangelischer Kirchentag in 1985 when he made it with the full force of his personality. What he had in mind was a lengthy and important assembly of official representatives of all the Christian churches, who were to speak with one voice in such a way that their word was heard and taken seriously throughout the world. He thought that such a council could be prepared for in two years, and should last for a year, and that the Protestant churches should invite the Catholic and Orthodox churches. His plea was supported by the grass roots in church communities and local groups. The call was taken up and widely approved. The Kirchentag declaration already speaks of the course of a conciliar *process*.[2]

From this prehistory it is easy to understand how the expression 'conciliar process' has persisted in German-speaking areas, though it was already dropped in the final Document of the European Ecumenical Assembly 'Peace in Justice' (Basel 1989) and replaced with the expression 'ecumenical process'. The Basel assembly is rightly regarded as a historic event, because official delegates from the Roman Catholic, Orthodox and Protestant churches of Europe took part in it. As is well known, it was arranged by the Conference of European Churches and the Council of the European Conferences of Bishops. In the account of its prehistory we can read that the 'preparation and implementation were a "conciliar process", though out of respect for some churches we have spoken of an "ecumenical process for justice, peace and the integrity of creation"'.[3] This formula also appears in texts of the working party which was formed to continue this process. In the preparatory group for the World Assembly at Seoul in 1990 on the same theme, the term 'conciliar process' was dropped at the request of the Catholic participants. However, it appears again in the Final Document, since this was the sole responsibility of the WCC (see below).

Are these recollections just word-games? I don't think so. The alterations express a change in understanding and evaluation. I think that what is at issue is the very question of the binding nature of this process, the commitments attached to it. Were some people afraid of the demand which is at least a connotation of 'conciliar'? Were we too near – dangerously near – to a council or unattainably remote from it? It is certainly significant that only the word 'process' has become firmly rooted, conceding that we are only, or already, or still, on the way and that even so successful an event as the Basel Assembly is only part of this way.

But back to the task set at Vancouver. There the word 'covenant' appears in brackets, and it is evidently meant to strengthen the term 'commitment'. At the 1990 World Assembly for Justice, Peace and the Integrity of Creation held in Seoul, in which unfortunately the Catholic Church took part with less commitment than in Basel (it did not join the WCC in issuing the invitations, was represented only by twenty advisers nominated by the Vatican, and shared in the preparation and the financing), after long debates covenant finally became a central concept. As it were over and above the obstacles of theology and church history, recourse was had to a good biblical concept. But even this intrinsically simple model was not understood and accepted everywhere. What was meant is that there is a covenant with us human beings from God's side – the covenant with Noah, with Abraham, with the people of Israel, leading to the new covenant in Jesus Christ – but that as partners in this covenant we human beings continually break it and violate it. In ancient Israel there was a ritual for renewing the covenant. Heino Falcke (at that time from East Germany) demonstrated in an article in the *Ecumenical Review* what elements formed part of this renewal: the recollection that from God's side this covenant is reliable and firm, the proclamation of God's will for his people, the rejection of false gods, the celebration of the covenant or its renewal, and the keeping open of the covenant. It was not meant to be exclusive but to represent an invitation. It was a bold undertaking in Seoul to understand the obligation to devote ourselves to justice, peace and the integrity of creation as the renewal and confirmation of our covenant with God and one another. The Seoul message stated: 'To give an adequate response to the global threats of today the churches need to discover new ways of giving expression to their universal calling. They need to live and to act as one body, transcending the boundaries of nations and at the same time breaking down the barriers of injustice by which Christ's body is dismembered today.'[4]

## The substance of the commitment

This 'new kind of commitment' was expressed in Basel in unanimous assent to a document which was very carefully prepared and worked out in partnership: it was discussed and accepted article by article in plenary session, according to a procedure worked out in advance. In Seoul, ten basic affirmations were made on the urgent problems of justice, peace and the integrity of creation. These are as it were themes which today are inescapable for Christians. In the message of the assembly they were summed up like this:

Now is the time when the ecumenical movement needs a greater sense of binding, mutual commitment and solidarity in word and action. It is the promise of God's covenant for our time and our world to which we respond. Thus we affirm:
— that all exercise of power is accountable to God;
— God's option for the poor;
— the equal value of all races and peoples;
— that male and female are created in the image of God;
— that truth is at the foundation of a community of free people;
— the peace of Jesus Christ;
— that creation is beloved of God;
— that the earth is the Lord's;
— the dignity and commitment of the younger generation;
— that human rights are given by God.

These affirmations, which of course are developed in more detail in the full text, have been described as an 'ecumenical social and ethical catechism'. Their content is the fruit of long ecumenical dialogues and discussions. So in substance they are nothing new; what is new is that they could command a consensus in Seoul.

The same is true of the four ways in which the covenant was made specific. The covenant was for:

— a just economic order and for liberation from the foreign debt bondage;
— the true security of all nations and peoples and for a non-violent culture;
— preserving the gift of the earth's atmosphere and for building culture that can live in harmony with creation's integrity;
— the eradication of racism and discrimination on all levels for all people, and for the dismantling of patterns of behaviour that perpetuate the sin of racism.

## Where the commitment applies

In my view this question is both the most difficult and also the one which is furthest from a solution. It has different facets. It was raised at every level of the conciliar process. Who is obligated to whom for what? Who in Europe committed themselves in Basel to the 100 articles of the Final Document which was accepted almost unanimously? What status does this document have in the churches and in public? The preface to the Basel report comments:

What is decisive is the reception of the events and perspectives by the churches in Europe themselves . . . It was the wish of many that the word of the European Ecumenical Assembly should be 'unmistakable'. The reference here was to words of Dietrich Bonhoeffer in 1934. To that it must be said that only the lifestyle of churches and Christians can be 'unmistakable'. This quality can only be achieved by an intense process of reception in which what has already been achieved is taken further and the degree of obligation and commitment grows. But that depends on the readiness of the members of the people of God to accept and develop what has happened.[5]

The same also, of course, holds for the world assembly.[6] There are two problems here: who can speak for the churches, and what weight even the most official church statements carry for church governments or church authorities at all levels and for members of congregations. Moreover, there is the question of the significance they have in public. For Europe in particular, this question is an urgent one. Most politicians and business-men, at least in Western Europe, but increasingly also in Eastern Europe, are members of Christian churches. We certainly will not reach them with papers but at most by the resistance (or the support) which grows out of experiences and formulations in the implementation of the conciliar process, e.g. actions to save creation, to preserve peace, or to achieve more justice in situations which are manifestly unjust (refugee policies, the withholding of rights from women, violence against women and children, etc.).

How difficult it is to apply general declarations of intent (obligations) in specific situations emerged in an important discussion at the Seventh General Assembly of the WCC in Canberra in February 1991. This was on a public statement to be made on the Gulf War. The very good analytical part of this document was followed by a series of appeals to the churches, to the UN, to states and politicians, etc. A German delegate proposed the insertion of a recommendation to the churches that 'they should abandon any ethical and theological justification for the use of military force both in war and in other forms of repressive security systems, and instead become advocates of peace'.[7] This recommendation was at first accepted, but then had to be withdrawn under pressure from primarily European delegates since otherwise the whole document would have been jeopardized. The text of the addition corresponded almost word for word with a recom-mendation from Seoul, viz., part of the covenant for demilitarization and non-violence. The old question whether there can be a 'just' or at least a 'justifiable' war became a point of dispute among Christians in the middle of the Gulf War. What obligation can there be if existing demands, arrived at in a laborious way, cannot help to achieve consensus over a tricky question even in so representative a body? In Canberra all that was left was a reference to a very general and pale recommendation of the Sixth General Assembly in 1983: 'The churches today are called on to confess their faith anew and to repent of their silence in the face of injustice and threats to peace . . .' At any rate that was no 'unmistakable' testimony in the face of the atrocities of the Gulf War!

A few days after the General Assembly in Canberra ended, the whole committee of the Conference of European churches and the council of the Conferences of Bishops met in Switzerland. They were considering the continuation of the ecumenical process in Europe and resolved to take it further. The following sentences are interesting in connection with the theme of commitment:

> While the Basel assembly achieved basic agreement in the sphere of 'Our common faith', it could not give conclusive answers to the many questions which the churches face in the area of the theme 'peace in justice' . . . In certain spheres there is still no consensus, e.g. on creating a non-violent culture or dealing with the social, cultural, economic and religious rights of minorities. Here ecumenical work after Basel is called for. Moreover, these questions and all the efforts to answer them show the urgent need to *take the ecumenical process further*.[8]

In the WCC, too, there are plans in this direction. That such further action is necessary is beyond dispute, but how it is to be achieved is still an open question. The new Central Committee elected in Canberra, which was meeting in September 1991, will have to decide on the next steps.

### Attempt at a summary

This can only be very personal.

1. The obligation not to break off the ecumenical ('conciliar') process is beyond dispute, at both the European and the world levels. That coincides with the desires and expectations of people at the 'grass roots' who are commited to justice, peace and the integrity of creation. But nowhere, at any rate in Europe, do they form the majority of church members, nor is it possible to ascertain how many bishops, church governments, synods, professors of theology and so on have really been fired by the thoughts and life of the conciliar process. There is still a long way to go, both within all the churches and in ecumenical thought and action. Even if I personally

am convinced that this process cannot be reversed because God's spirit is at work in it despite all the problems, it will not win through 'by itself'. It needs prayer, work, a sense of 'commitment' among all concerned at every level.

2. These levels must not be played off against one another. Neither in Basel nor in Seoul was there a satisfactory solution to the problem of the mutual support of official representatives of the churches and the groups and movements often passionately engaged in the process. In Basel, highly-qualified hearings on specific issues were arranged outside the official discussions. Where the assembly met, on the ground floor there was the 'Workshop for Europe's Future', multicoloured and with many themes and actions, while above the delegates were meeting in working parties and plenary sessions and making their decisions without taking into account the views expressed from 'below'. In Seoul, the preparatory group attempted by appeals to motivate the churches to appoint as delegates 'those who are engaged in the real struggle' and those who are 'involved'. This met with only partial success. Instead, large numbers of such people came as visitors or with press cards. What went on here at the highest level accords with the reality in many churches and groups. Here, too, there is more a juxtaposition than a collaboration of church governments, church authorities, and groups and movements acting independently. These are usually ecumenical, which often means that confessional frontiers no longer play any role. They are sometimes in contact with one another regionally, nationally or internationally ('networked' or associated) and are often more deeply involved in the conciliar process than the official bodies. Mutual information, cross-fertilization and acknowledgment are urgent.

3. In further work the two terms 'conciliar' and 'covenant' should not disappear. A mere 'ecumenical process' seems to me to be too little. The word 'conciliar' continues to exert pressure towards the full unity of churches and Christians. The hope that they/we will one day really speak 'unmistakable' words with one voice on all the threats of our time and act accordingly still remains. The element of obligation can best be taken up within the framework of the covenant or a variety of covenants. Human beings enter into obligations before God to remain in the covenant. They also enter into obligations with one another; they are accountable to God and to one another. Strictly speaking, only persons can enter into obligations. Even if the situation in church law were different, only those present in Basel and Seoul put themselves under an obligation. But in doing so they also took on the obligation of handing on the content of the covenant to those around them. No one can work out just what that involves. But at least I would like to pass on one experience at Seoul which was significant for me. On the day after the assembly a Korean theologian

who had already played an active part in the preparatory group said: 'Now it's all different. Now we are in covenant.'

4. The indissoluable link between justice, peace and the integrity of creation must remain obligatory. At the latest, the Gulf War has shown with inexorable clarity how they belong together; how war and new injustice grow from injustices of various kinds; how war destroys human life physically and psychologically and causes environmental catastrophes of unforeseeable extent. In the building up of a 'new' Europe it remains to be seen what churches and Christians feel themselves obligated to. The European 'fortress' or the European 'home'? Pride or penitence at the festivities over the so-called discovery of America? Will this be a Europe for justice or simply the strongest economic power which is interested only in its own profit and its own security?

5. Lastly, there remains the question of the source of the obligation in the conciliar process and how it can be kept alive. For me it grows from the belief that God's covenant means life and creates life. Life is always life in community; life is being incorporated into God's creation and into the fellowship of love lived by and in Jesus Christ. Without love for life, without fellowship with brothers and sisters, for me there is no obligation. This love transforms into prayer and action anger and suffering at the injustice and violence that happens and that also lives in me. That is how 'obligation' is lived out.

I would like to end with a doxology which stands at the end of the Seoul report.

> Having committed ourselves in covenant solidarity and
> Mindful that we are stewards of creation
> We join with all You made
> To celebrate your glory
> And to sing your praise.
>
> Glory to God
> Who in the beginning created all things
> And saw that it was good.
>
> Glory to Jesus,
> Firstborn of the new Creation,
> And Redeemer of all.
>
> Glory to the Holy Spirit
> Who in the beginning hovered over the water
> And who fills Creation with Your love.

*Translated by John Bowden*

## Notes

1. See *Gathered for Life*, the official report of the Sixth Assembly of the WCC, Geneva 1983.

2. *Deutscher Evangelischer Kirchentag, Düsseldorf 1985, Dokumente*, Stuttgart 1986, 585.

3. *Frieden in Gerechtigkeit. Die offiziellen Dokumente der Europäischen Oekumenischen Versammlung 1989 in Basel*, Zurich 1990, 26f.

4. Seoul Documents, cyclostyled, 1990.

5. *Frieden in Gerechtigkeit* (n. 3.), 31f.

6. Quoted from a newspaper account .

7. Minutes of the meeting, available from the Conference of European Churches, PO Box 2100, CH1211 Geneva 2, Switzerland.

8. Seoul Report (n. 4)

# Contributors

JON SOBRINO was born in the Basque country in 1938. He joined the Jesuits in 1956 and has been a member of the Province of Central America since 1957, living mostly in El Salvador; he was ordained priest in 1969. He took a first degree in philosophy and literature at St Louis University in 1963, a master's in engineering at St Louis in 1965, and gained his doctorate in theology in Frankfurt in 1975. Among many published works, those translated into English include *Christology at the Crossroads* (1978); *The True Church and the Poor* (1984), and *Jesus in Latin America* (1986).

MARY GREY was born in the North of England in 1941 and studied classics and philosophy at Oxford (MA) and theology at Louvain (PhD). She has taught theology and philosophy of religion at St Mary's College, Strawberry Hill, London, and is now Professor of Feminism and Christianity at the Catholic University of Nijmegen, The Netherlands, and President of the European Society for Women in Theological Research. Publications include *Redeeming the Dream: Feminism, Redemption and Christianity*, London 1989; *From Barriers to Community: The Challenge of the Gospel for a Divided Society*, London 1990, and many articles on fundamental concepts of theology from a feminist perspective of interconnectedness.

OTTMAR JOHN was born in Herford, Westphalia, in 1953. He gained his doctorate in 1983 and his MPhil in 1985, both in Münster. He is at present assistant at the fundamental theology seminar in the university there.

WOLFGANG KESSLER was born in 1953. He is a sociologist specializing in economics and social science and is political and economic editor of the journal *Publik Forum*. He lives in Oberursel, Germany.

DIETER LUTZ was born in Gaildorf, Germany, in 1949. He studied law and political science in Germany and abroad, gaining doctorates in social science in Tübingen and in political science in Nijmegen. Since 1976 he has been deputy academic director and also administrative director of the Institute for Peace Studies in Hamburg.

JACQUES AUDINET was born in 1928 and studied at the Institut Catholique in Paris, the Sorbonne and the University of Chicago. He has been professor at the Institut Catholique (1969) and director of the Institut Supérieur de Pastorale Catechetique (1969–1975) and is now professor at the University of Metz.

LUKAS VISCHER is Professor of Ecumenical Theology in the Evangelical-Reformed Theological Faculty of the University of Bern and head of an ecumenical institute of the Protestant churches in Switzerland; from 1961 to 1979 he was Director of the Faith and Order Commission of the World Council of Churches. His work has focussed on the confession, ecumenical dialogue and ecclesiology, and in recent years above all on the conciliar Movement for Justice, Peace and the Integrity of Creation. He has edited two conference reports on this theme: *Rechte künftiger Generationen, Rechte der Natur*, Bern 1990, and *Die Rolle der Kirchen beim Schutz der Erdatmosphäre*, Bern 1991.

JAN KERKHOFS was born in 1924 and was consecrated priest in the Jesuit order in 1956; he taught moral theology in Louvain and sociology in Antwerp. From 1963 to 1981 he was Secretary-General of the international foundation Pro Mundi Vita. He is Professor Emeritus of Pastoral Theology in the University of Louvain. He is also Co-Chair of the Steering Committee of the European Value Systems Study Group and, since 1966, international spiritual adviser to Uniapac (an international Christian organization for employers). His publications include *De Kerk in Vlaanderen* (1982), *Morgan is er al* (1976), *De stille Ommekeer* (= *L'Univers des Belges*) (1984) and *De smalle weg* (1988).

JACQUES GAILLOT was born in Saint-Dizier, France, in 1935, and trained at the seminary of Langres. He then spent two years in Algeria and after studies in Rome and ordination in 1961 taught at the Liturgical Institute in Paris and the seminary of Chalons, moving on in 1965 to the regional seminary of Champagne. In 1968 he was put in charge of the institute for training teachers of the clergy and in 1973 nominated vicar general of the diocese of Langres. He was consecrated bishop of Evreux in 1982.

JOHANN BAPTIST METZ was born in Auerbach, Bavaria, in 1928 and consecrated priest in 1954. He has doctorates in both philosophy and theology and is currently Professor of Fundamental Theology in the University of Münster. Of his many publications, *Theology of the World* (1969) and *Faith in History and Society* are available in English; his most recent books are *Lateinamerika und Europa: Dialog der Theologien* (1988); *Welches Christentum hat Zukunft?* (1990); *Gottespassion* (1991); and *Augen für die Anderen* (1991).

DAVID TRACY was born in 1939 in Yonkers, New York. He is a priest of the diocese of Bridgeport, Connecticut, and a Doctor of Theology of the Gregorian University, Rome. He is the Greeley Distinguished Service Professor of Philosophical Theology at the Divinity School of the University of Chicago and the author of *The Achievement of Bernard Lonergan* (1970), *Blessed Rage for Order: New Pluralism in Theology* (1975), *The Analogical Imagination* (1980) and *Plurality and Ambiguity* (1987).

MARGA BÜHRIG is well known for her meditations on Swiss radio and for articles on the theme of 'Justice, Peace and the Safeguarding of Creation'. She gained her doctorate in German and history, and went on to study Protestant theology. She works as a teacher and a journalist, and has been Director of a Protestant Academy in Zurich. From 1983 to 1991 she was one of the seven Presidents of the World Council of Churches and from 1988–1990 she was Moderator of the preparatory group for the Seoul Assembly on Justice, Peace and the Safeguarding of Creation. Her books include *Die unsichtbare Frau und der Gott der Väter* (1987) and *Spät habe ich gelernt, gerne Frau zu Sein. Eine feministische Autobiographie* (1987).

# Members of the Advisory Committee for Practical Theology

*Directors*

| | | |
|---|---|---|
| Norbert Greinacher | Tübingen | Germany |
| Norbert Mette | Münster | Germany |

*Members*

| | | |
|---|---|---|
| Carlos Abaitua | Vitoria | Spain |
| Rosemary Crumlin RSM | Victoria | Australia |
| Virgil Elizondo | San Antonio, Texas | USA |
| Segundo Galilea | Santiago | Chile |
| Alfonso Gregory | Rio de Janeiro | Brazil |
| Frans Haarsma | Nijmegen | Netherlands |
| Adrian Hastings | Leeds | England |
| François Houtart | Louvain-la-Neuve | Belgium |
| Jan Kerkhofs SJ | Louvain-Heverlee | Belgium |
| Hubert Lepargneur OP | São Paulo | Brazil |
| Anthony Lobo SJ | Washington DC | USA |
| Thomas Nyiri | Budapest | Hungary |
| Emile Pin | Poughkeepsie, NY | USA |
| †Karl Rahner SJ | Innsbruck | Austria |
| Rosemary Radford Ruether | Evanston, Ill | USA |
| Sidbe Semporé | Cotonou | Republic of Benin |
| Francisco Soto | Jalapa, Veracruz | Mexico |
| Yorick Spiegel | Frankfurt am Main | Germany |
| Wevitavidanelage Don Sylvester | Galle | Sri Lanka |
| Rolf Zerfass | Höchberg | Germany |

## Other Issues of *Concilium* published in 1992

### Towards the African Synod
edited by G. Alberigo and A. Ngindu Mushete

Offered as resource material in connection with the planned African Synod, and with many African writers, this focusses on the rich historical heritage of the African synodical tradition; surveys the situation of the churches in many African countries, not least in the face of the challenge from Islam; examines the African economic and political scene; traces what has so far been done (and not done) by way of preparation for the synod .

1992/1    February

### Fundamentalism in the World's Religions
edited by Hans Küng and Jürgen Moltmann

Begins by defining fundamentalism from both a theological and sociological perspective; looks at the challenge of contemporary Jewish and Muslim and Christian (Orthodox, Catholic and Protestant) fundamentalism and possible answers to it; discusses the relationship of fundamentalism to both modernity and postmodernity.

1992/3    June

### God, Where are You? A Cry in the Night
edited by Christian Duquoc and Casiano Florestán

Studies especially the silence of God in the modern world. It examines the absence of God in the Bible; in the experience of Jewish poets; in sickness; in the suffering of women, the exploited and the humiliated; in distress arising from sin and in death; and looks at the significance of this silence for church institutions.

1992/4    August

### The Taboo on Democracy in the Church
edited by James Provost and Knut Walf

It is widely held that democracy is incompatible with the nature of the Catholic Church. This issue questions that assumption by examining both democracy and the nature of the church. It considers the ecclesiological implications of the theme; gives examples of democratic structures; and makes concrete proposals for the future.

1992/5    October

### The Debate on Modernity
edited by Claude Geffré and Jean-Pierre Jossua

It is widely said that the modern world is now a thing of the past; we have now moved on to post-modernity. This issue looks at definitions of modernity and its relationship to Christianity; at the rise of post-modernity and criticisms of it; and at possible Christian strategies in the face of the crisis for modernity.

1992/6    December